PIONEERS OF EAGLE ROCK

PIONEERS OF EAGLE ROCK

Edited by Eric H. Warren *and* Frank F. Parrello

THE History PRESS

Published by The History Press
Charleston, SC 29403
www.historypress.net

Cover images: Front: Grading the Eagle Rock Road in the canyon below the Rock in about 1900. *This item is reproduced by the permission of the Huntington Library, San Marino, California*; one of many souvenir postcards of the Eagle Rock. The eagle shadow has been enhanced. *Courtesy of the Stargel Collection*. Back: The Whites and their neighbors are planting onions. William White is the second from the left. The Whitney girls are setting out the onions. Lottie White holds her dog at the right. The ranch buildings are in the middle distance. *Courtesy of the Elena Frackelton Murdock family.*

First published 2014

Manufactured in the United States

ISBN 978.1.60949.827.6

Library of Congress CIP data applied for.

Notice: The information in this book is true and complete to the best of our knowledge. It is offered without guarantee on the part of the authors or The History Press. The authors and The History Press disclaim all liability in connection with the use of this book.

We dedicate this book to Jack Forbes and Mrs. C.W. (Emma Elinor) Young, as well as to the many people who have loved and created Eagle Rock, its spirit and its history. We have relied on their work in this and our other efforts to remember and carry on our community history.

Jack Forbes

Chants rise
from the Eagle Rock
as we
in the dark
on the cool granite surface
count stars
chart galaxies
dream up lives.

Valley of Indians
Eagle Rock Valley
still in the 1800s
only Native People
living there
along tree-lined streams
and lush springs.

Now the Indians
have returned
majority once again
from Mexico this time
brown skins
with Filipinos
and a world of others
along Eagle Rock Boulevard
waiting for green lights.

...

Eagle Rock
the spirit is still there
somehow
in Mother Earth
when you can see
snow-covered Mt. Wilson
on a clear day
the spirit
of the Eagle
is still there.

¡El Aguila vive!

Excerpt from "Memorias de Eagle Rock" by Jack D. Forbes ERHS S'59 July 29, 1992

A Native American writer, scholar and political activist, Forbes died in 2011.

Born on January 7, 1934, Jack Forbes lived an eventful life and left behind a visible and profound legacy. He earned his PhD in history from the University of Southern California in 1959, with a doctoral dissertation, "The Apache, Navajo, and Spaniard," that was published in 1960. Forbes went on to write numerous books and journal articles.

In 1970, Jack co-founded Deganawidah-Quertzalcoatl University, more commonly known as DQ University. California's only tribal college, located near Davis, California, it still exists. Native America now has thirty-five tribal colleges, which enroll approximately 33 percent of the Native American postsecondary population. All were founded as a result of Forbes's tireless efforts on behalf of Native American history.

Jack was a proud son of Eagle Rock and a longtime member of the Eagle Rock Valley Historical Society.

This formal portrait shows an impressive Emma Elinor Young, with the Youngs' adopted daughter, Amber, in 1906, the year they arrived in Eagle Rock. *Courtesy of the Louanna Clark, Emma Young Collection.*

Mrs. C.W. Young

Not least among the attractions of the City of Eagle Rock is its history which dates back to the beginning and rates among the first things of the history of California.

This priceless legacy of romance and adventure is being appreciated more and more by people who have the destiny of our little city, as a sacred trust not to be disregarded or neglected.

We believe in the adage of that great man, Gladstone, "Show me a people that remembers its past and I will show you a people that can be trusted with the future of a city or nation."

Excerpt from "History of Eagle Rock Filled with Adventure, Romance and Politics," by Mrs. C.W. (Emma Elinor) Young

Mrs. Young was a pioneer clubwoman, historian, lecturer and authority on California history and landmarks. For more than fifty years, she urged Californians to preserve their heritage. Her love of pageantry and reenactment caught the attention of many children and adults in Eagle Rock, teaching them, gently, the importance of the past.

Mrs. Young was born Emma Elinor Hine on May 27, 1869, in Geneseo, Illinois, and grew up on a farm there. The youngest of eight children, she went to Northwest Normal School, taught school and participated in the kindergarten movement when it started in this country. She was the principal of Annawan School for many years.

On November 23, 1899, Emma married Charles W. Young in Geneseo. They left Illinois, and in 1906, they located in Eagle Rock. There they purchased the Ellis home, a three-story Victorian farmhouse built in 1888. They called the house Castle Crags.

Mr. Young was a founding member of the City of Eagle Rock Board of Trustees, the second mayor and, for many years, its city clerk. Before and after Mr. Young's death from diabetes, their home was a center of social life, frequented by authors, sculptors, actors and civic leaders.

CONTENTS

Acknowledgements	13
Introduction	15
Part I. The Land, the First People and the Legend	17
Part II. Spanish, Mexicans and Californios	27
Part III. The Great Partition	43
Part IV. Farmers and Villagers	61
Part V. Dreamers and Schemers	82
Part VI. Eagle Rock City	104
Afterword	135
Sources	137
About the Editors	143

ACKNOWLEDGEMENTS

We wish to thank photoshop artist Amy Inoye; transcribers Mary Denardo of "Girl Friday," Connie Hood and Deborah Huntington; the staff of the Huntington Library; Don Crocker; Occidental College Library Special Collections; Katie Taylor; Jane Tsong; Charles Fisher; Oran Asa; Historic Resources Group; Pasadena Museum of History; the *Eagle Rock Sentinel*; our editors with The History Press, Jerry Roberts and Ryan Finn; and the California Digital Newspaper Collection, University of California–Riverside. Much of the information and many of the photographs in this book were collected by the members of the Eagle Rock Valley Historical Society; we thank our colleagues and predecessors.

Special thanks from Eric to Karen, my wife, lover and sometime copy editor who aids and abets my periodic fits of creativity.

Special thanks from Frank to Heather Hoggan for all your love and support.

All uncredited photographs are from the Eagle Rock Valley Historical Society's collection.

INTRODUCTION

As in most of America's Southwest, three different civilizations have prevailed in the Eagle Rock area. Ironically, the longest era, that of the first people to live on this land, is the least known. The process of conquest was inevitably brutal, abetted by disease, and the conqueror often ignored the adaptations of his predecessors to the land. The Spanish, Mexican and Californio era is somewhat more known, but there is relatively little detail about individuals and their lives. When the labor and achievements of the conquered were no longer respected, the memory of the past could be romanticized as legend or simple and carefree pageantry.

As the concept of Eagle Rock and probably even the name for the geographical feature goes back only to the beginnings of American dominance, we include in our history those who owned or occupied parts of the community of today. The first people's environment and customs will be considered. The Verdugo family's Rancho San Rafael dominates the Spanish history. The Great Partition included the territory that was transferred to Beaudry, to Glassell and Chapman and to Dreyfus. We will focus on Eagle Rock City, but we will also consider the adjoining areas, which are now accepted as being in Eagle Rock.

We thank the pioneers of Eagle Rock history for amassing the wonderful resources from which we had to draw. We quote these historians extensively and suggest that the reader consult the original documents to find a broader view of our history than can be contained in this short volume. We have tried to make our sources clear in the chapter notes at the end of the book.

It is the pioneers, chroniclers, developers and visionaries whom we have to thank for the remarkable persistence of the community of Eagle Rock as a focus for the loyalty and collective efforts of its citizens. We are still here, relevant and innovative, amid the great and diverse metropolis that is Los Angeles.

Authors' note: Many of the street names used in historic Eagle Rock have changed. It will be our practice to use contemporary names in our writing. When quoting others, the original names will be used. On their first use, the current name will be given in parentheses (or brackets if present in a quote).

PART I

THE LAND, THE FIRST PEOPLE AND THE LEGEND

An Indian baby lay on a skin. An Eagle swooped, clutched the babe and flew eastward. The Indians in chase, called to the Sun, "Let him crush himself against the Rock and turn to stone upon it." 'Twas done, the infant lay unhurt below.
—"Indian Legend," published around 1970 by the Eagle Rock High School Jazz Band

THE LAND

Bernice Johnston was a charter member of the Eagle Rock Valley Historical Society and wrote the first book on *California's Gabrielino Indians*, published by the Southwest Museum in 1962 and based on the notes of John Peabody Harrington, archaeologist, ethnologist and linguist. She begins her description of the valleys that became Eagle Rock thus:

> *Long ago, before the twentieth century sealed the earth with concrete and asphalt, before it drained all the winter run-off to the sea, there existed in Eagle Rock Valley many a source of sweet water, most of them forgotten, and many a small pool or swamp where it collected. In very ancient times prehistoric animals lapped from the edges of a lake just below what is now the intersection of York and Eagle Rock Boulevards.*

In 1939, when Sparkletts excavated for a new building in its complex near Lincoln Avenue, a nearly complete mammoth skeleton was discovered. The tusk and part of the skull are visible here at center right. The remains have joined many others in storage at the County Museum of Natural History.

This postcard shows the how Eagle Rock and its surroundings looked before modern development. There are wires to the right of the Rock leading from the Pacific Power and Light Substation that reveal the date to be after 1911.

While the Rock was the symbol, water was essential to life in the valley. The stream that flows from between the Eagle Rock and the hills to the west was the source of the most prominent water features in the valley. It can still be seen in several places before it disappears into the storm drain system. This flow was joined by streams from the canyons now occupied by La Loma Road and Monte Benito Road and pooled south of the intersection of La Loma Road and Figueroa Street. Out of this pool flowed a braided stream down Yosemite Drive, once Sycamore Avenue, named for the riparian trees that once lined its banks. The stream continued to just east of Eagle Rock Boulevard, where it was joined by water bubbling from the springs located south of Colorado Boulevard and Argus Drive next to the hills. The stream flowed down the valley to a low spot near Colorado and York Boulevards, where it formed a swampy area. Rising ground impeded drainage to the Los Angeles River except in extremely wet years.

As is still the case, rainfall in the area was extremely variable. In dry years, little water was visible. In wet, the valley bottoms became raging torrents, excavating new channels and washing away any obstacles in their path.

Faulting, which runs generally from east to west, causes the springs and the high water table that are still encountered by excavators in the valley. The areas between the faults are filled with gravel and rock basins, which accumulate water. Water is thus present near the surface but not lower in the rock. As this pooling is relatively shallow, it is subject to considerable seasonal and year-to-year variation depending on rainfall.

The Eagle Rock and other exposed rock formations are also the result of the active geology of the region. Geologist Giuseppe Cugno wrote:

> *Several hypotheses have been formulated through the ages to explain the rather unusual appearance of the rock exposure and erosional features. These hypotheses have varied from ancient stories of Indian lore and legend to current scientific explanations of which I will give you a brief general explanation. I have to admit that the old legends and stories of the Eagle Rock may be more appealing to the fantasy and imagination than the cold but still interesting scientific explanations.*
>
> *The Eagle Rock from which our community takes its name is located at the northeastern portion of the city of Los Angeles near its boundary with the city of Pasadena to the east. Similar rock exposures are present in various areas of Eagle Rock, but none are as large or as visible or have such unusual features. The same rock formations are visible along Figueroa Boulevard as well as in the hills south of the Eagle Rock Plaza* [see photo of Pelican Rock on page 62].

The formation comprising the Eagle Rock and almost all the hills in the area north of York Boulevard extends to several other areas of the Los Angeles Basin, particularly Topanga from where the typical section was described and mapped. In Eagle Rock, it consists of a mixture of sand, gravel and cobbles that were deposited in the Middle Miocene (10 to 15 million years ago). The conglomerate and sandstone units are deposited in a shallow marine, high-energy environment, and several fish fossils found in the bedrock have been used to date the time of deposition.

Vertical uplift, coupled with differential cementation, erosion, and other weathering processes, has created the topography of the Eagle Rock as the Indians originally saw it centuries ago. Erosional process such as the wind, possibly coupled with a process called spalling, has created the unusual shape along the west side of the otherwise semi-spherical rock exposure.

The First People of Eagle Rock

Bernice Eastman Johnston recounted:

Quite early men passed this way. Little is known of them and there is not even a legend to prove that any remained here when, about two thousand years ago, bands of other Indians began threading the mountain passes from the deserts, to settle on these coastal plains.

These were the tribesmen whose villages dotted the land when the Spanish came to settle it. We call them the Gabrielinos from Mission San Gabriel, which was founded in 1771. Since the language of the whole area, from below Malibu to below Laguna and back to a vague border beyond Riverside, was closely related, all of the people are covered by the term Gabrieleno, which is a "working" title, non-Indian.

Recently, the name Tongva has been generally adopted as the term for this group of Native Americans. This name, too, is controversial. Andrew Salas, chairman of the Gabrieleno Band of Mission Indians/Kizh Tribe, stated:

The Kizh (pronounced "keetch") were known to themselves and to other tribes of outside origins as the people of the willow branch, tule and brush houses. Before 1771 Spanish encountered the Kizh and conquered and enslaved them...During this time the Spanish renamed the Kizh "Kichirenos"...The Gabrielino Band of Mission Indians/Kizh Tribe does not recognize the made up title Tongva.

Johnston continued:

The language was a dialect of Shoshonean but we cannot call these Indians "Shoshones." That term is reserved for more distant related tribes. Many of the neighbors of the Gabrielenos, in the mountains, deserts and along the coast, also spoke Shoshonean but those of the Ventura–Santa Barbara region and of San Diego County were not related in this way.

We have no valid record that any of our predecessors noticed what seems so obvious to us, the likeness of a great bird in flight that gives Eagle Rock Valley its modern name. The Spanish dubbed this landmark "Piedra Gorda," the "Fat Rock." Among the descriptive place names told to anthropologists when there were still old Gabrielinos who knew the language, none applied to this area.

Salas said:

The history I am going to give you is oral history that has been passed down for generations. The way the city of Eagle Rock was named was for the large rock, which stands in the middle of the city known today as Eagle Rock. My people were the first to call the area (Ah-sowt-To-tah), which means golden eagle rock, because of the natural formation which looks like the face and wings of a nearly extinct golden eagle that frequented that area.

Johnston continued:

One is not able to state exactly how many separate villages existed in this valley. The stone pots and mortars that were found in such profusion many years ago have been scattered without records being kept. A few were dug up near Colorado and Mount Royal, not too distant from a flowing spring that is still remembered. Such a spring still exists on the grounds of Occidental College; and one may imagine that another ideal location lay in the canyon below the Eagle Rock itself.

While availability of water spelled limits to the size of a settlement, Eagle Rock Valley was rich in other resources. Willows and rushes for framing and thatching the round huts, bard wood and reeds for arrows, massive oaks to yield a bountiful harvest of acorns for the staples mush and bread, all these abounded.

The steeper hillsides were thickly covered with the low trees and bushes the Spanish were to name the "chaparral." These grew a few inches during the winter rainy seasons and guarded themselves during the arid summers with their hard bark, thick, fuzzy leaves and thorns; but here, in leaf, root, bark, fruit and berry, the Indians found food, medicine, material of hot and cold drinks and chewing gum, as well as for baskets, mats, dyes, tools and weapons. Lowly weeds such as the nettles gave fibers for tough, fine string and rope. The yucca had innumerable uses.

Sunny fields of native grasses, not yet displaced by the Mediterranean wild oat, yielded seeds to be toasted in flat baskets with hot stones. Spring flowers, poppies and wild roses were woven into garlands and hair ornaments.

Trade was brisk between the villagers of the inland valleys and the coast and with those of the islands where Gabrieleno-speaking Indians lived. Dried fish and dried venison made a mutually welcome change of diet for the inland hunters and their seaward-oriented tribesmen. Steatite (soapstone) from Catalina was a prized item. Where an even exchange could be agreed upon, small, thick beads of clam shell were measured by strings of them wound about the fist for units of "money." Shells were also used for necklaces, bracelets, ear bobs and hair ornaments.

While each village, with few exceptions, had its own political organization, all were tied in a loose ceremonial union. Professional messengers were kept busy going from chief to chief to make arrangements for reciprocal celebrations of ceremonies or taking and returning gifts according to a set scheme of protocol.

No enemies from beyond their borders menaced these people; but occasionally a feud developed between two villages, perhaps over a gift not correctly returned, or the stealing of a woman. Annual "battles" of name-calling and threats might finally lead to a short but deadly "war" which possibly cleared the air between such enemies. However, peace was the normal thing.

It is unlikely that we shall ever know the names of the villages, large or small, of Eagle Rock Valley. Their people were most probably absorbed very early into the life of San Gabriel or San Fernando Mission. The records of baptism and confirmation carry many names (Christian names of Spanish origin), each followed by that of the Indian Village of birth. The puzzle remains, in by far the larger number of these, as to where the villages were located. Using data from history, tradition and archeology it has as far been possible to relate name and place for less than a hundred of what must have been several times that many Gabrielino settlements.

The records of deaths at the missions often reveal a pitiful length of continued life after birth or confirmation. European diseases began the decimation among both children and adults, with the first years of existence of these institutions. This continued after the missions closed and the remnant of the tribe scattered out to obtain pittances by working for men who now owned the land upon which the almost forgotten villages had once flourished. Since wages on the ranches were often paid in the form of raw grape brandy another death soon diminished even that remnant. This practice continued after the coming of the North American, with the result that there are few individuals alive today who can call themselves Gabrielinos and these are, for the most part, not full-bloods and have no knowledge of the language of the rich heritage of song and ritual.

This tragic story is shared by the Gabrielenos who once roamed Eagle Rock Valley. Long ago they disappeared as though they had never had those many hundreds of years of well-adapted living along these beautiful slopes. It is well that we now have enough knowledge of their ways so we can refute the canards of those who wanted us to believe (because of ignorance or their own guilt in the matter) that these Indians were lazy, dirty and "low in the scale."

We should remember that it was part of their daily ritual to go down to river or pool or spring to bathe, every morning before the sun came up, so that the gentle Wiyot (and not the vengeful Chungichnish) "would see them clean." And when we toss a glance, in our rapid passage, at the "Eagle Rock" we should remember that the eagle was somehow a symbol of the indestructibility of the human spirit, and the Rock itself was undoubtedly one of the "First People," transformed at the time of the new creation from the earlier folk of a dim and ancient time."

For many years, native people survived by blending into the larger population. Since the 1960s, pride in native cultures and origins has become understood as important to people's engagement in the larger world. This has given rise to the revival of nearly extinct cultures and languages. Coupled with increased economic opportunity, this revival has prompted the creation of several political organizations representing factions of the Gabrielino/Tongva/Kizh people.

LEGENDS OF THE EAGLE ROCK

Many of the early historians of the valley, most prominently Emma Young, attributed legends about the rock to native peoples. The phrasing of these legends, which shows a lack of knowledge of native culture, makes these associations quite doubtful in our view. This romantic approach to the past was quite popular throughout the nation, and similar legends were promulgated about several other Eagle Rocks. Francis J. Johnston, in his first comprehensive history of Eagle Rock, noted the following:

> *Unfortunately there seems to be a great dearth of information relating to any tales of Indian origin despite the fact that an Indian campsite is known to have existed within two miles of the natural edifice. Remains of this village were found on the Campbell-Johnson Ranch, which, during the 1880's included the Rock, and the area known to the Spanish Californians as El Varganzo now covered by northeastern Highland Park and Southern Eagle Rock. However it would appear that at least one legend was taken down and recorded by some of the mission fathers at San Gabriel. But this ancient myth was somehow passed over when the history of the region was being chronicled and is not now to be found in any formal document. The author of this present paper, therefore, is indebted to friends who remember having heard it from a teacher by the name of Mrs. Hamer some years ago at Eagle Rock High School.*
>
> *The story runs in this manner. In the years before the coming of the white man to California an Indian clan made an annual habitat of the ground at the base of the great Rock. The young chief of this band had committed a great sin in the eyes of his father by marrying out of the clan, taking to wife a girl from a neighboring group, which used to be located at the other end of the valley under Pelican Rock. Unforgiving to the end the old man died and was reincarnated as a giant eagle who was given to dwell near the site of his son's encampment at the Rock. The huge bird still held within his heart the smoldering hate once felt by the old father for his son. During the first stay of the clan at the Rock, after the old chiefs death, the young wife of the new chief each afternoon laid her first born child on a blanket in the sun to receive the benefits of its rays.*
>
> *One day while flying above the village the reincarnated old man, desiring to inflict punishment on his people, noted the boy and swept down at a tremendous speed to seize him up in his talons. The warriors of the band*

> *on witnessing this act, caught up their weapons and a few among them, by virtue of superb marksmanship, were able to wound the tyrant of the skies forcing him to release the child who fell unharmed into a clump of sagebrush. The great bird struggled mightily to raise himself above the missiles of the warrior but the initial wounds had weakened him and, though not slackening speed, he was unable to gain altitude. His tremendous wings cut giant arcs, his great muscles strained to their utmost, but it was no use, he hurtled headlong into the bald face of the great Rock with such terrific impact that an impression of himself in frantic flight was incised thereon which has remained to this day.*
>
> *Such was the ancient Indian tale explaining the impression that had so little effect on the Californios that they named it Piedra Gorda or Big Rock.*

Some say that the overhang forming the right wing of the spread-eagle shadow has been eroded or broken off over the years. The photographic evidence, beginning in 1888, is quite inconclusive. Many images have been retouched to enhance the eagle shadow.

Johnston continued the romantic tradition in his chapter "Pageantary Past." Although there is no evidence for any of this, as Emma Young might have said, "It makes a good story":

> *The young Shoshone brave stirred uncomfortably, the day was hot and to insure concealment he was forced to lie flat on his stomach against the hard stone surface of his observation point which overlooked the beautiful rolling valley of Haleamuepet. He had been stationed here by his chief who was trying to verify the report scouts had brought into the tribal encampment, as it lay under the great sycamores in the river wash below the hills bordering this valley on the east and south, that the strange white conquistadors, who were known to have conquered all the lands of the fierce Aztecs to the far south, were actually coming into this region to establish their strange village. Fifteen summers ago a party of these people had been seen marching near this valley, but their only intent then seemed to have been to get away to the settlement they had made on the borders of that great desert region which used to protect this quiet land from invasions…the whites called their place San Diego…*
>
> *If this brave had been closer to the two men in broad hats and leather jackets bearing lances, carbines and pistols, he might have overheard these words:*
>
> *"There, Sanchez, lies in the most beautiful spot of what will be my rancho; there we will till the soil and raise corn, barley, and beans; I will herd my sheep here too and some of my cattle."*

"It was in 1772 that my eyes first encompassed this valley and the other territory that will be my rancho. It was while I was on mail-courier duty from the Presidio de San Diego to the Presidio de Monterey that I passed this way and on seeing this vast stretch of fertile land knew that should we of Spain see fit to continue our colonization of this California I would claim this as my own."

"Si, corporal Verdugo, it is indeed beautiful, more so than our Sonora, I shall be happy working for you when, and if, you get your rancho, but had we not better return to the camp near the Pueblo de Los Angeles else some of the wild savages here about may deftly remove our hair?"

"You speak with the tongue of a senora, not that of a soldier of Spain, Sanchez. The Indians here are not dangerous; has there ever been any trouble at the missions or the new Pueblo? Nonsense! But come, we shall return, I trust our caravan will continue soon on its way to Monterey for it is there, from Comandante Pedro Fages, that I must secure permission to turn my cattle, now at Mission San Gabriel, out to graze on these hills and valleys."

PART II

SPANISH, MEXICANS AND CALIFORNIOS

Historian John R. Kielbasa sets the scene for the beginnings of the rancho period with more information about the local Native American settlements and another opinion about the significance of the Eagle Rock:

> *The story of Rancho San Rafael begins with the Indians who first lived in the area. The Gabrielino village of Hahamogna was located within the wide spread boundary lines of the rancho. Early accounts place Hahamogna along the banks of the Arroyo Seco near Garfias Springs. It was at the intake of "La Zanja," an irrigation ditch used by Verdugo. Rancho San Rafael was referred to the early Spanish as Rancho La Zanja (Ranch of the Ditch) because of the extensive irrigation system there…*
>
> *Significant amounts of Gabrielino artifacts were found in Verdugo Canyon, along Chevy Chase Drive at the base of the foothills and along the west bank of the Arroyo Seco (Dry Stream)…But, the site most significant to the Gabrielinos can be located off the north side of the Ventura Freeway (134) where North Figueroa Street ends. Here, a large rock formation resembles an eagle in flight. Known to the Spanish as "Piedra Gorda" or "Fat Rock," this outcropping has no known Indian name. The eagle had strong cultural and religious influence upon the Gabrielinos and the site was often visited by them in order to pay homage to the bird's likeness. Today, it is known as Eagle Rock, and although eroded by the elements over the years, the resemblance to an eagle is still apparent.*

JOSE MARIA VERDUGO

According to records at the Mission San Gabriel recorded at the time of his marriage, Jose Maria Verdugo was born in Loreto, Baja California, in 1751 to Juan Diego Verdugo and Maria Ignacia Carillo. (The Spanish pronunciation of the initial *V* sounds closer to the English *B*.)

Kielbasa recounted the Verdugos' military service:

> *There were two brothers who enlisted in the Royal Spanish Army at Loreto, Mexico in the 1760s. In 1769 they were part of the forty leather jacket soldiers assigned to protect the first land expedition into Alta California. Jose Maria Verdugo and Mariano de la Cruz Verdugo were both privates when they arrived in San Diego under the command of Captain Fernando de Rivera y Moncada. After fifty days of arduous marching from La Paz they reached San Diego on May 14, 1769. Their mission was to establish the first colony of New Spain in the frontier of Upper California. The brothers would spend the rest of their long military careers in the new frontier, but at separate posts…*
>
> *Jose Maria Verdugo was assigned to the San Diego Presidio under the command of Pedro Fages. When the Mission San Gabriel was founded in 1771, he was promoted to corporal and placed in charge of the "escolta" or the Mission Guard. The original location was near the present Whittier Narrows on the Indian village site of Sigba-Na. Almost four years later, due to a flood, the mission was moved to its present location…This small detachment remained under the authority of the San Diego Company. In 1779, at 28, Verdugo married Maria de la Encarnacion Lopez at the San Gabriel Mission…*
>
> *While at San Gabriel, Corporal Verdugo took part in sporadic campaigns against renegade Indians. One revolt in particular occurred on the night of October 25, 1785. Verdugo learned beforehand of a heinous plot conspired by local Indian neophytes to murder the mission's two padres and the eight-man guard. He and former fellow trooper, Manuel Nieto, devised a clever ruse and were able to capture ten Indians inside the mission compound without firing a shot, and not a single arrow was slung during the attack.*

The revolt referred to was that led by Toypurina, a shaman wise in the ways of her people. A "novice" at the mission, Nicolas Jose, had asked her, after an appropriate gift, to lead a revolt against the Spanish. Nicolas had

The first painting of a California mission shows Mission San Gabriel in 1832. It is in a narrative style, showing activities around the mission. The typical architecture of the first people, men in traditional dress and women in mission style are shown at lower right. In the left rear are native convert labor quarters. *Courtesy of the Santa Barbara Mission Archive Library, painting by Ferdinand Deppe, detail.*

done his best to fit in with the conquerors but had become disillusioned with their prohibition of appropriate mourning for his dead son.

Toypurina and her associates were taken for trial to San Juan Bautista before Governor Fages. Jose Verdugo was a witness. The conspirators were asked ten questions, several of which were attempts to discover the extent of the conspiracy. Fages was undoubtedly aware of how greatly his troops were outnumbered. A rebellion led by a leader with standing among many natives was of great concern. None of the conspirators acknowledged responsibility or guilt.

Toypurina was exiled to San Juan Bautista and forced to marry a Spaniard. The only known female leader of a native rebellion refused to confess her "sin" at the time of her death.

In the early 1780s, Corporal Verdugo undertook to supplement his meager and precarious salary by grazing a substantial number of horses and cattle on the fertile lowlands through which the San Gabriel River found its way to the sea. The land was already preempted by his comrades Nieto and Dominguez, and he was compelled to move his stock to another range. In 1784, Verdugo learned that Juan Jose Dominguez had received a substantial grant from Commandante Pedro Fages, the military governor of Alta California. Known as Rancho San Pedro, the seventy-four-thousand-acre grant was the first in California. Noting the grant to Dominguez, Verdugo filed a petition with Fages for his own. Occidental College professor Robert Glass Cleland related:

> *To avoid trespassing upon either mission or pueblo lands, Verdugo chose an unoccupied tract west of the watercourse called indiscriminately the Arroyo Hondo and the Arroyo Seco. The land lay about a league and a half from the San Gabriel Mission, on the old "Road to Monterey." From this junction of the road and the arroyo, the tract extended "to the river of the Pueblo de la Reina de Los Angeles as far as the Saca de Agua (or water dam) and north to the Sierra."*
>
> *Fages replied on October 20, 1874: "I concede to the petitioner the permission which he solicits to keep his cattle & Horses at the 'Arroyo Hondo'... provided that he does not prejudice the...Mission, nor the inhabitants of the Reina de Los Angeles, & having some one in charge, without being exposed to the gentile Indians, nor in any manner injuring them."*

Henry Welcome, the founding president of the Eagle Rock Valley Historical Society, commented:

> *The Rancho was called "Paraje de Zanja de Zacamutin" (the place of the Zacamutin ditch, recognizing the importance of irrigation to agriculture in the dry country). Rancho San Rafael, as it was later called, appeared on the 1836 Los Angeles census as Rancho de los Verdugos.*
>
> *In November 1789, one month after Pedro Fages granted the land to his faithful soldiers, the Governor wrote his superiors in Mexico for approval of his grants to Dominguez, Nieto and Verdugo. Through a legal opinion of Galindo Navarro in Chihuahua, dated October 27, 1785, the three grants were approved.*
>
> *Along with the grant, there was an understanding that Verdugo would raise 2000 head of stock, build a stone house and provide "two fanagas of grain for the good of the community." A fanega is 1.6 bushels.*

Kielbasa continued:

> *Corporal Verdugo was unable to settle upon his newly acquired property. In his stead, he sent his brother Mariano, who had retired from the army*

in 1787 presumably due to a disability. Mariano built a crude house of sticks, cultivated a garden, and laid out a vineyard. During this period of retirement, Mariano served as alcalde (mayor) of Los Angeles from 1790 to 1793, then again in 1802.

Jose Maria had retired from active duty but continued as a captain of the guard at the San Gabriel Mission. He did not set himself up as proprietor of his domain, perhaps because investigations were underway to choose a site for a new mission. In August of 1895 the governor sent out a commission whose object was to select a mission site between San Gabriel and San Buenaventura. Its report read in part "The first thing we met on the rancho of Cpl. Verdugo was a great field of watermelons, sugarmelons and beans, with a patch of corn."

As luck would have it for Verdugo the commission did not select any of the area encompassed by his rancho, in all probability because there were no permanent structures on the property then. Instead they took over the rancho and supporting buildings in the possession of Francisco Reyes, a "squatter" on land, which belonged to the Mission San Gabriel out on the far side of the San Fernando Valley. There the Mission San Fernando Rey de Espana was established in 1797.

In 1799, Governor Borica gave Verdugo the right to use his own cattle brand, a low armed "Y" atop a horizontal "9." This indicated that Jose Maria's livestock had become sufficiently numerous to raise him to the status of a true ranchero. For "it was not the custom of the Spanish government to give a brand to a man unless he had one hundred and fifty head of breeding cattle."

Cleland continued:

As the years went by, Verdugo became a victim of dropsy [an abnormal accumulation of fluid under the skin] *and found himself unable to endure the hardship of army life. He suffered, too, from the great misfortune, as he somewhat ambiguously declared, of having "five daughters and one small male child, but no son to assist me." Provincial regulations required a soldier incapacitated by illness…to live in one of the pueblos; but Verdugo pointed out that in a pueblo he would "have to suffer the various fatigues which all persons, although for good, share in common," and then added, "I know that I am already incapable. I require some greater ease."*

The leisure-seeking corporal accordingly petitioned Governor Diego Borica, who has assumed office in 1794, for a confirmation of the grant

> *which "Colonel Don Pedro Fages" had originally approved in 1784, and asked permission to retire from the army and make his home on "the tract of the Zanja." Verdugo added that the ranch was already supporting perhaps "two hundred head of horned cattle, three hundred horses and one hundred and fifty sheep."*
>
> *Governor Borica submitted Verdugo's petition to Lieutenant Antonio Grajera for verification and comment...Upon receipt of Grajera's reply, Borica formally approved Verdugo's petition, and at the same time commended him for having fulfilled the conditions of the earlier Fages' concession which required him to stock the grant with cattle, cultivate part of the land, and build dams and ditches for irrigation. In conclusion, the governor counseled Verdugo "to increase the breed of his sheep and not to prejudice the neighboring Missions and to treat well the Indians both Christians and Gentiles that live near the Rancho, with that love and charity so much recommended by the laws, but not on this account to forbear living with the proper precaution so as to avoid all insult."*
>
> *Having obtained an honorable discharge from the army in 1799, Verdugo went to live upon the grant that he had been awarded fifteen years before. With him he took his numerous daughters, his "one small male child," and his lingering dropsy. In the course of the years, the "Invalid with the Grade of Corporal," and the relatives who came to live with him, cultivated some of the most fertile parts of the Rancho San Rafael and brought a considerable area under irrigation. By 1817 the ranch was pasturing 1,800 head of large cattle, 1,000 calves, 600 unbroken horses, 70 tame horses, and 70 mules. Twelve years later the number of cattle had almost doubled.*

Glendale historian E. Caswell Perry offered more detail about life on the Rancho, perhaps due to his friendship with Dora Verdugo, who still lived in Glendale at the time he was writing:

> *Verdugo was a conscientious and faithful worker. Even with the necessity of using primitive implements such as a wooden plow, he cultivated many acres. The grain was thrashed in the most ancient of ways, by having the cattle trample it, and then winnowing it by tossing it into the wind. Verdugo was able to supply grain for export to Mexican ports.*
>
> *Additionally he grew grapes and made wine, besides growing vegetables, including red peppers, a staple of the Spanish diet.* [Actually, such peppers were American in origin and are little used in the cuisine of

> Spain.] *Among other crops grown at San Rafael Rancho were pomegranates, figs, peaches, pears, apples, oranges, limes and other citrus fruits.*

Some credit for this must be given to the laborers employed by Verdugo, mostly unskilled and mission-trained natives in this era and less lucky immigrants from Mexico, probably of the same polyglot stock as the Pobladores, founders of the nearby Pueblo de Los Angeles.

Perry continued:

> *The good life lived by Don Jose on his extensive rancho was by no means confined to agriculture, viticulture and the raising of cattle, horses and sheep. Life during the days of the Dons contained more than its share of adventure. Deer, antelope, wild horses, and even grizzly bears and mountain lions provided a variety of hunting and sports.*
>
> *Scattered over the rancho, Don Jose had a number of adobe buildings for temporary seasonal use. He was apparently somewhat haphazard in his building practices, as some of the structures which he called "homes" were without roofs and otherwise incomplete. This was not as slipshod as it appears on the surface, the buildings remained in that condition because they were in use only in good weather...The more or less permanent home of the family was located in what today is northwest Glendale, having been mentioned on numerous occasions in court records and other documents of the last one hundred twenty years.*

Other sources mention an adobe built near the wet area in the western York Valley. The permanent water there allowed the growth of large fields of garbanzo beans.

> *It is apparent that those living at Rancho San Rafael must have had frequent contact with persons from the outside world, even if only for brief periods. It was the custom of the era when visitors of consequence were expected for a mounted guard, headed by Don Jose himself, to meet and greet the guests at the rancho boundaries and provide an escort up to the hacienda itself. One can almost see the former corporal in his new and more imposing role as a California Don, making his guests welcome, entertaining them lavishly and creating an atmosphere of indulgent hospitality...*
>
> *The family tree, as shown in Dora Verdugo's records, tells us that Don Jose, a native of Spain, married Maria Lopez of Sinaloa, Mexico, and that they were the parents of these children: Julio, Catalina, Maria*

> *Josefa, Maria Ignacia and Maria Antonia. Julio, the grandfather of Dora Verdugo, married Maria de Jesus Romero, of Santa Barbara and their children included Dora's father Teodoro.*

Cleland wrote of the impending end of Don Jose's life:

> *Despite the dropsy and frequent bleedings (which, according to common report, constituted an excellent remedy "for a pain in the side, with fresh drinks taken moderately"), Jose Maria Verdugo lived more than thirty years after his retirement as an invalid from the army. In 1828, when death at last seemed imminent, he gathered his failing strength, summoned the appropriate officials, and made his will.*
>
> *The document, like all wills of the old Spanish-Californians, was strikingly naïve, intimate, and detailed. It began with the usual affirmation of faith:*
>
> *"In the name of God and his Most holy Mother, Our Lady conceived in Grace, and without any original sin…considering that men have to die and that such may take place at any hour, without knowing when, firmly believing as I do in the Mystery of the Most Holy Trinity, the Father, Son and the Holy Ghost, three persons distinct, and one only true God & in all and everything that our Holy Mother Church believes and acknowledges. The Most Holy Mary being my intercessor and advocate…as she has been my whole life, I order and make my testament in the following form."*
>
> *Thereafter, item by item, came the bequests, large and small, and the list of debts, down to the last fraction of a peso, which the testator owed to others, as well as those which others owed to him. The will of Jose Maria Verdugo clearly reflected the psychology and simple social background of the early Californians.*
>
> *The instrument also specified that Catalina was to receive the vineyard and that the fruit trees were to be divided equally between her and Julio. Bequests of livestock and a good deal of personal property were parceled out among his kin.*

It seems reasonable to assume that this disposition reflected Julio's status as the only son, as well as Catalina's situation. Blinded by smallpox as a child, she could not care for herself. This enumeration also reflects the lack of actual cash available to even the richest at the time. A system of barter and debt by notation prevailed, as no one could actually settle debts with money. This situation would prove a great liability when the money economy of the English-speaking invaders required payment rather than the word of a gentleman.

Perry described the end of Verdugo's life:

> *Don Jose had reached four score years when he died on April 12, 1831. His remains were interred in the cemetery of Mission San Gabriel. Although mission records bear testimony to such burial in the original cemetery next to the mission church, no marker is there today to indicate the exact spot. It seems reasonable to assume that his wife, Maria de la Encarnacion, was also buried there.*
>
> *Verdugo's will mentioned numerous previous gifts to his daughters Maria Josefa and Maria Ignacia (Maria Antonia had died), an obvious attempt to explain why he left the rancho to only Julio and Catalina. Notwithstanding, the two married daughters contested the will. When it came out in open court that they had been dealt with generously by their father during their lifetimes, the court upheld the terms…The amicable spirit in which they accepted the ruling indicated that they were as interested in having…the will interpreted by competent authority as in upsetting it. At that time and place in history, even many people of consequence could not read or write, a situation that brought about a natural suspicion of written documents. The daughters were also quoted as remarking that they had never even seen the will.*

By this time, several momentous changes had occurred—even though they little affected life on the remote rancho, they would have important consequences. On September 27, 1821, the independence of the Mexican Empire was proclaimed. After several attempts at reconquering Mexico, Spain recognized its independence on December 28, 1836. Thus, Jose Maria Verdugo died a citizen of the Mexican Empire, and his children became citizens of the Mexican Republic.

The Mexican Congress passed "An Act for the Secularization of the Missions of California" on August 17, 1833. The act also promoted the further colonization of both Baja and Alta California, the expenses to be borne by the proceeds gained from the sale of mission property to private interests.

In 1895, journalist and historian Charles Fletcher Lummis criticized the act and its results:

> *Disestablishment—a polite term for robbery—by Mexico (rather than by native Californians misrepresenting the Mexican government) in 1834, was the death blow of the mission system. The lands were confiscated; the buildings were sold for beggarly sums, and often for beggarly purposes. The Indian converts were scattered and starved out; the noble buildings were pillaged for their tiles and adobes.*

The results for the remaining mission Indians were devastating. Even though the population had diminished considerably through disease and the Franciscan practice of cloistering women of childbearing age, they were still considered by the padres to be humans with souls worth saving. Secularization deprived Native Americans of all of their possessions, land and cattle. They were, in effect, dehumanized and left an impoverished labor force subject to exploitation.

JULIO AND CATALINA VERDUGO

E. Caswell Perry resumed:

> *With the death of Don Jose, his son, Julio, then 42, took over the role as landed don. Riding was his favorite hobby, and he was fond of wearing the picturesque costume of the California aristocracy. He also enjoyed having a long train of relatives, guests, and servants following, as he rode over his rancho, looking after the many business interests now left in his care.*
>
> *Perhaps the most accurate description of Julio, which has come down to us is the observation of a contemporary, Jose Olivas, a native Angelino who came to the rancho San Rafael in 1865 and was frequently Julio's house guest. He described him as "a little short man, who wore leggings and short trousers open at the side and decked with silver buttons." He added the fact that Julio customarily rode a large black horse…*
>
> *From other pioneer residents, one often heard of Julio's custom in obtaining seasonal labor, usually for planting and harvesting his crops and looking over his live stock. He used native Indians for the purpose. They were available because they lived in nearby villages—one in la Canada Rancho, in Canada Valley and another in the area, which is the site of Sunland Tujunga today.*
>
> *In the years 1831, 1833, and 1836, Don Julio was alcalde for the rancho, and served as juez di campo in 1840, the latter title being regarded as a unique honor as it involved temporary authority over fellow Californians of equal social status and wealth during their assembly for one of their annual cattle roundups.*
>
> *…Julio fathered nine sons, and took them with him on his daily horseback tours of the rancho as soon as they grew big enough to sit astride*

> *a horse and stay upright in the saddle. He and his wife, the former Maria Jesus Romero, also had two daughters. The nine sons were of considerable assistance in the raising of wheat, beans, corn, barley and hay, and also in tending large herds of cattle and strings of horses. There were pens and a dairy at the cienega as early as 1835.*
>
> *Don Julio's building activity was a sure sign that he was keeping a sharp eye on rancho business. In 1833, he put up a house on a hilltop on the southern part of the rancho, naming it Las Garbanzos (later Garvanza), in honor of the garbanzos or chickpeas he was growing nearby.*

Henry Welcome commented:

> *A number of years ago I located a huge and very ancient olive tree on Fisher St., which is just a sidewalk running at right angle to Meridian St. The olive is about one half block north of Luther Burbank Junior High. I have no proof but feel this is the approximate location of Julio's home in Garvanza.*

An adobe house was built in Verdugo Canyon in about 1828. Perry quoted Dora Verdugo, his daughter:

> *Mystery surrounds the building of the ancient adobe house on Bonita Drive in Verdugo Woodlands. Don Jose, his daughter, Catalina, and his son, Julio, have all been named at one time or another as its builder. However, Dora Verdugo was born in the Bonita house and spent her childhood there. She has emphatically stated that this adobe was put up by her father, Teodoro, son of Julio, and was owned by him up to the time of his death on June 2, 1904. At no time was it owned by Catalina, his aunt, nor by any other person.*
>
> *"Of course, Catalina lived there for a long time," Dora Verdugo once declared..."*

Teodoro and Catalina retained ownership of the house and the land around it after the Great Partition.

Alta California Is Conquered, Prosperity Ensues

Although no member of the Verdugo family is known to have participated, an event occurred on and near the rancho that led directly to the surrender of Californio troops to the United States Army and the end of the Mexican-American War in Alta California. The Californios were known as gallant fighters and superb horsemen but hardly amenable to the kind of military discipline necessary to organize really effective resistance to the invaders. Warrant Officer 1 Mark K. Denger wrote the story for the California State Military Museum:

> *In January of 1847, the last two serious military engagements against U.S. forces invading California were fought at the battles of San Gabriel and La Mesa just below Los Angeles. Gen. Flores, seeing the situation as hopeless, now moved north of the city. In the meantime, Frémont arrived in the Los Angeles area from the north.*
>
> *It was on January 11, 1847, a few miles above San Fernando, that Col. Frémont received a message from Gen. Kearny informing him of the defeat of the enemy and the capture of Los Angeles. That night Frémont's battalion encamped in the mission buildings at San Fernando. From the mission Col. Frémont sent Jesus Pico to find the California army and open negotiations with its leaders. Jesus Pico, a cousin of Gen. Andres Pico, found the advance guard of the Californians encamped on the Verdugo Ranch.*
>
> *Detained there, Pico informed the leading officers of the army of Frémont's arrival and the number of his men. With the combined forces of Frémont and Stockton, now in Los Angeles, he urged them to surrender to Frémont as they could obtain better terms from him than from Stockton.*

This conference is said to have taken place under the tree in Verdugo canyon now known as the Pico oak.

> *The commissioners met in the deserted ranch-house of Tomas Feliz (Campo de Cahuenga), and a treaty was drawn up.*
>
> *The principal conditions of the treaty of "Capitulation of Cahuenga," as it was termed, were that the Californians, on delivering up their artillery*

Catalina and Teodoro Verdugo's home in Verdugo canyon is pictured at the right rear. In the foreground is the Pico oak. The home still stands on Bonita Street in Glendale. *Courtesy of the Glendale Public Library Special Collections.*

and public arms, and promising not to again take up arms during the war, and conforming to the laws and regulations of the United States, shall be allowed to peaceably return to their homes. They were to be allowed the same rights and privileges as are allowed to citizens of the United States, and were not to be compelled to take an oath of allegiance until a treaty of peace was signed between the United States and Mexico, and were given the privilege of leaving the country if they so wished to do so.

BOOM AND BUST

The Sierra Gold Rush had created tremendous demand for meat. Cattle were driven north to the gold fields, leaving few behind to breed. Despite the hazards of the drive, great profits could be made, according to Cleland:

> *The rise in cattle prices which began early in 1849, continued with only temporary setbacks for nearly seven years. During that time, beef cattle were quoted as high as $75 in San Francisco and small calves brought from $20 to $25 each. Even on the distant southern ranges, the price of full-grown steers, representing an eight or ten fold increase over that of the hide and tallow days, rose to $30 and $40 a head.*
>
> *But the fat years of inflated prices and treacherous prosperity proved, in the end, the curse of the native landowner. "Curious tales of the improvidence of Californians in those last days," wrote Charles Nordhoff in 1873. "Saddles trimmed with solid silver, spurs of gold, bridles with silver chains, were among the fancies of the men: and a lady in Santa Barbara amused me by describing the old adobe houses, with earthen floors covered by costly rugs;...and the senora and senoritas dragging trains of massive silk and satin over the earthen floor." It must have been an odd mixture of squalor and splendor.*

By the end of the 1850s, the bubble had burst. In 1861, the rains came shortly before Christmas and continued almost without cessation for nearly a month. The rivers washed away waterworks and vineyards. The lowlands flooded, Southern California was isolated and thousands of cattle drowned. The next year, luxuriant grass grew, but the great flood of 1861–62 was followed by two years of unparalleled drought. A virulent epidemic of smallpox began in 1862.

Welcome continued:

> *In 1852, the U.S. Board of Land Commissioners was created to investigate California land titles. The Verdugos presented their claim to the commission. An American friend of the family, lawyer Joseph Lancaster Brent, represented them and the Board confirmed their claim on September 11, 1855. They were very fortunate in having Brent, as many titles were not confirmed, only confirmed in part or the owner paid nearly as much as the value of the land to dishonest American attorneys for their grants...*

> *In 1855, the same year the United States Land Commission confirmed the Rancho San Raphael title, Julio sold Brent 671 acres…just east of the Los Angeles River and just across from Griffith Park. Brent paid $4,000. In 1857, the Verdugos traded 4600 acres in the Burbank area, to a Jonathan Scott for Rancho La Canada. This 5745-acre ranch became the property of Catalina. Not far east of the present intersection of Acacia Street and Verdugo Road was Portosuelo. Julio built an adobe for his wife Maria about 1860.*
>
> *Apparently the Verdugos needed money to construct Portosuelo for on January 2, 1861, they mortgaged the Rancho for $3,445.37. A Jacob Elias held the paper. At the time the interest rates were usurious; this loan cost the Verdugos three per cent per month. That April Julio and Catalina finally followed their father's will and legally divided the rancho. The blind sister took the northern half and her brother the southern portion. The dividing line started a little north of where Los Feliz Blvd. now crosses the Los Angeles River and ran diagonally north of east bisecting the Eagle Rock (then still called Piedra Gorda). This dividing line terminated at the Arroyo Seco, the eastern boundary of the rancho. In 1863, Elias foreclosed on Julio for non-payment. The following year he was awarded judgment of $10,795. Verdugo contested the decision and irrevocably lost in a court decision in 1869. By this time the debt had risen to $58,750 from $3,445 in eight years.*
>
> *Verdugo could not meet this great loss and was forced to put Rancho San Raphael up for public auction. Alfred B. Chapman, a lawyer, purchased the property at the sheriff's sale for the amount of the debt. He received the deed a few months later.*

Julio had borrowed money from folks who didn't play by the rules of honor between gentlemen to which he was accustomed. The fate of the Verdugos' rancho was decided by a legal system that had arrived with an ever-increasing horde of invaders (now governors). The Americans had come to paradise and taken ownership.

James Miller Guinn offered this sketch of the rancho's new owner in the biographical volume of his *History of California*:

> *Alfred Beck Chapman was born at Greensboro, Ala., September 6, 1829. He graduated from West Point in 1854, and was later stationed at various western points…It was in 1861 that he came to Los Angeles to make his home, studying law with his father in law J.R. Scott. After the war he*

formed a partnership with Andrew Glassell…Later Mr. Chapman, who had won his way to high favor with his constituency by his straightforward methods and his unusual ability in unraveling knotty problems, was elected city attorney, and later still district attorney, serving in both capacities with great satisfaction to the general public. Together with Mr. Glassell, he owned at one time ten thousand acres in Orange County and thereon they laid out the town of Orange, promoting and developing this beautiful little city. In 1879 he retired from the active pursuit of his profession and took up the life of the farmer, settling upon a portion of the Santa Anita rancho.

PART III

THE GREAT PARTITION

Definition and Division

Henry Welcome reported in his article on the Verdugos:

> *The true legal boundaries (of the Rancho) were not laid down until the United States Land Commission gave the title to Verdugo's heirs. G. Howard Thompson, the United States Commission surveyor, plotted the rancho in 1871. He found it to contain 36,403 acres. A legal description placed before the U.S. Land Commission at that time was as follows:*
>
> *Commencing at the source of the Arroyo Hondo (Arroyo Seco where Devils Gate Dam now stands. H.W.), which Arroyo crosses the old road running from the mission of San Gabriel to Monterey at the distance of about one and one half leagues. From the mission, said boundary line running from the source of said Arroyo down said stream to its mouth at the river of the Pueblo of Los Angeles, thence up the river last mentioned to the place where said river issues from the Sierra at the mountain called Cahuenga; thence in a Northerly direction from said mountain at the point last mentioned to the Cerrito Colorado, and from thence to the place of beginning.*
>
> *This area includes the present communities of Burbank, Glendale, Highland Park, Mt. Washington, Flintridge, Montrose and parts of Pasadena, La Crescenta and La Canada. All of Eagle Rock lies within its boundaries.*

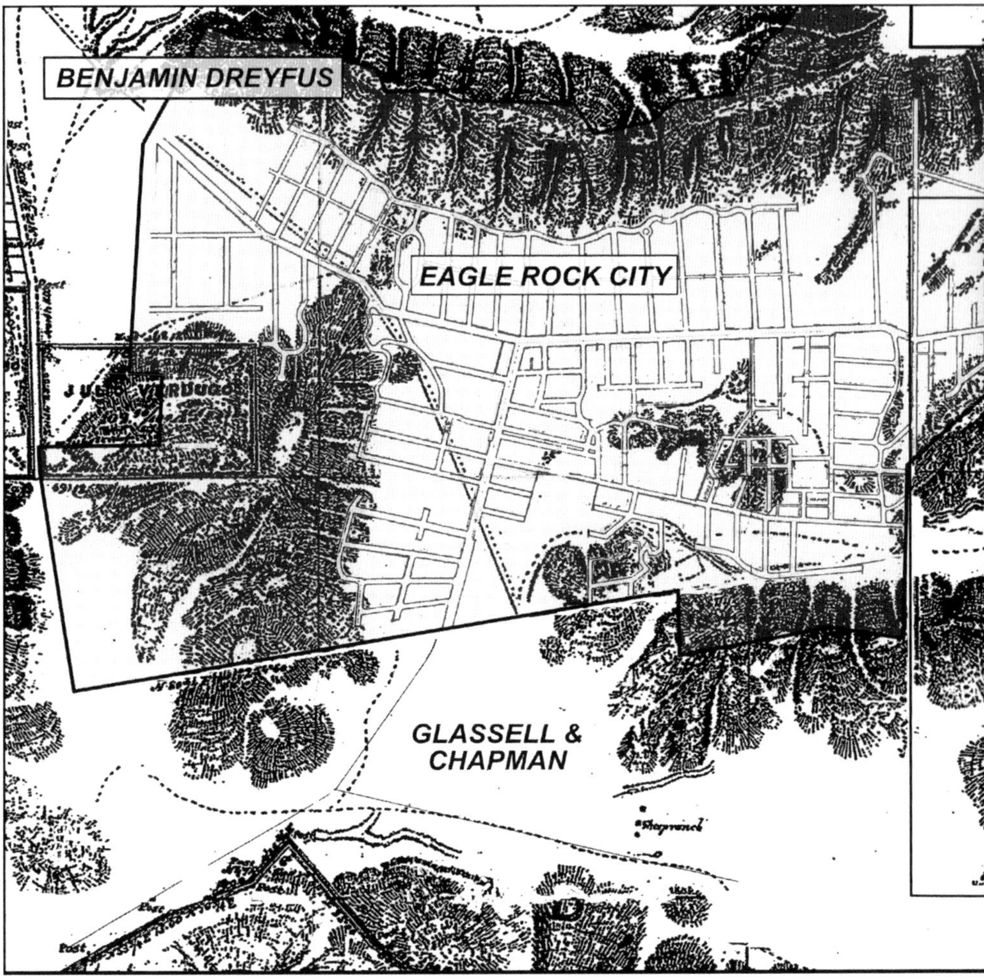

Although intended to clarify the Verdugo's title to the Rancho San Rafael, this survey and detailed description were made just in time to facilitate its division. Welcome continued:

> *The great Rancho San Raphael had already been encumbered by Julio and Catalina through debts and lawyers, fees, leaving Chapman only the recourse of a court suit to settle the affair. Chapman, Andrew Glassell, and others (perhaps Smith, another law partner. H.W.) brought suit, naming thirty-six defendants; the resulting decision in 1871 was to divide the Rancho into thirty-one parcels among twenty-eight persons. The largest award went*

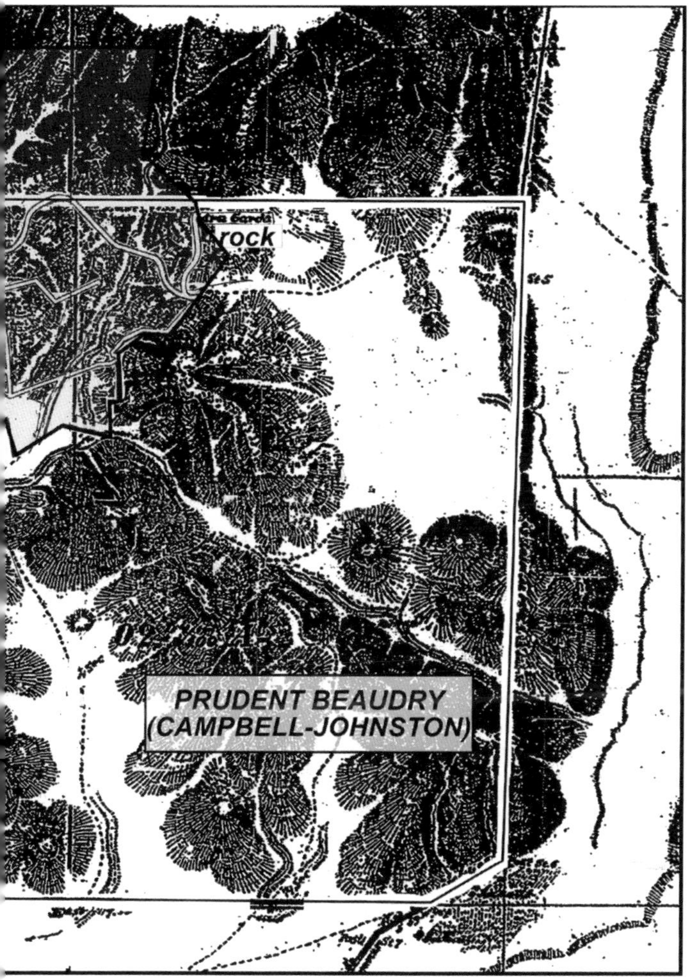

The underlying map shows a part of the rancho in 1871. The topography of the area can be clearly seen. The partition as it affected the valley and the future boundaries and streets of the city of Eagle Rock are overlaid.

to Benjamin Dreyfus. This was for 8,000 acres and included most of Eagle Rock City and the southern corner of Glendale, later called Tropico. Catalina and her nephew Theodoro Verdugo, were awarded 3,000 acres and Julio retained Portosuelo with its two-hundred acres. Several other members of the Verdugo family received acreages.

Two other parcels that are part of today's Eagle Rock were distributed. The area to the south, including the York Valley, went to Chapman and his partner, Andrew Glassell. The area to the east went to Prudent Beaudry.

The "Discontented '70s"

In its transition from quasi-feudalism to American boomtown, Los Angeles and its surroundings were beset by turbulent times. Welcome recounted:

> *The quarter-century following the United States conquest was a rather lawless one in Southern California and the second-most famous bandit of the period has an association with the Eagle Rock. Tiburcio Vasquez attained great notoriety over the state before his capture in 1874 and locations which he frequented are of considerable local celebrity. He was captured about ten miles west of Los Angeles (now Hollywood) and the following day he gave a lengthy statement of his career to a reporter for the Los Angeles Star, which was printed in the issue for May 16, 1874. In April, Vasquez was using the ranch house of George Allen as a hide-out…Vasquez, being short of funds, sent a young Mexican named Lebrado Corona to "case" the ranchos for a possible robbery. In a few days Corona returned, reporting that… Alexander Repetto had recently sold a large quantity of wool.*
>
> *Vasquez and his party left Greek George's house on April 11, 1874, crossed the Hollywood Hills into the San Fernando Valley on horseback. They rode to the Pacoima area and thence via Tujunga and La Canada to the foot of the Eagle Rock. Here they camped for the night. The following day Vasquez rode to the Repetto ranch alone. Finding a sheepherder of Repetto's, Vasquez informed him that he had lost a horse and offered $15 for its return. Riding on and not finding Repetto home he checked the ranch out for himself and by a round-about route returned to the camp below the Eagle Rock. I quote Vasquez:*
>
> *"As soon as it was dark I returned with my men to the neighborhood of Repetto's and camped within a few rods of the house. The next morning about breakfast time we wrapped our guns in our blankets, retaining only our pistols, and I went toward the house, where I met the sheepherder and commenced talking about business. If Repetto wanted herders or shearers, how many sheep could he shear in a day, etc., speaking in a loud tone, in order to let Repetto hear us and throw him off his guard. I had left my men behind a small fence and being told that he was at home, I entered the house to see if I could bring the patron to terms without killing him. I told him I was an expert sheep shearer, and asked if he wished to employ any shearers; the gentlemen who were out waiting by the fence were all good shearers, and wanted work. All were invited in, and as they entered surrounded Repetto.*

I then told him I wanted money. At this he commenced hollering, when I had him securely tied, and told him to give me what money he had in the house. He handed me eighty dollars. I had told him that that would not do; that I knew about his affairs; that he had sold nearly $10,000 worth of sheep lately, and that he must have plenty of money buried around the house somewhere."

"...Repetto then protested that he had paid out nearly all the money he had received in the purchase of land; that he had receipts to show for it, etc. I told him that I could read and write and understood accounts, that if he produced his books and receipts and they balanced according to his statements, I would excuse him. He produced the books, and after examining them carefully, I became convinced that he had told me nearly the truth. I then expressed my regrets for the trouble I had put him to, and offered a compromise. I told him I was in need of money, and asked if he would accommodate. He kindly consented to do so and sent a messenger to Los Angeles for the money, being first warned that in the event of treachery and betrayal his life would be forfeit."

The messenger was a thirteen-year-old boy, the nephew of Repetto. The boy presented a check for eight hundred dollars in his uncle's name to the cashier of the Temple and Workman Bank. The teller could see the youngster was greatly agitated but the boy would admit to nothing and the check was found good. The cashier communicated his suspicions to the bank president, Mr. Temple. The lad, frightened for his uncle's life, insisted on the money, of which five hundred in gold was given to him, and he promptly returned to the ranch. Within thirty minutes the Sheriff had gotten together a posse and was on his way.

The three bandits took to the road, with only a three-mile start on Sheriff Rowland's posse. They headed north and west through some land on the east bank of the Arroyo Seco within the present limits of Pasadena.

As the bandits approached the Arroyo they came upon a wagon driven by Charles Miles, Superintendent of the Los Angeles Water Co., and two companions, John Osbourne and John Rhodes. Vasquez relieved the three of about seventy-five dollars and a five dollar gold watch from Miles. The robbery took but moments and the Mexicans were soon on their way to where the Arroyo Seco enters the mountains.

Crossing the stream in the present bed of the Devil's Gate Reservoir, they fired some shots into the air. The guide failed to appear, and the posse was getting much closer. With no choice Vasquez and his two companions found the trail, which led up the side of the Arroyo. At the summit the trail ended.

The three bandits started down the canyon wall of Clear Creek, soon giving up their horses and footing it down the wash until they came into the Big Tujunga. As darkness came to the mountainsides, Sheriff Rowland called off the manhunt and returned with his men to Los Angeles.

Rowland and a small posse captured Vasquez several days later at the home of Greek George. Though the bandit was seriously wounded when taken, he recovered to stand trial in San Jose. A hangman ended his 21-year career of crime, which ran from armed robbery to murder, Friday, March 18, 1875. Sheriff Billy Rowland received a reward of $8,000.00 plus $43.25 for "expenses."

Soon after, in the winter of 1876, Archduke Ludwig Salvator of Austria traveled through the Los Angeles area. He was born on August 4, 1847, in Florence, the fourth son of Leopold II, Grand Duke of Tuscany and Princess Mary Antonietta of Borbó-Dues Sicilies. Throughout his life, he had an illness called elephantiasis that made it difficult to get up and move about without help. An educated, handsome person who learned fourteen different languages, including Greek and Latin, he dedicated most of his life to traveling. He described his journey along the Los Angeles River Valley and up the Verdugo wash thus:

Continuing on to the right the way leads to Portesuelo, with its cornfields and scattered houses, then past the Cañada de Francisco María [the most westerly canyon in the Chevy Chase district in Glendale], *so-called from a treacherous Indian who lived down in a gully and was greatly feared by his neighbors. These unpleasant memories are soon dispelled, however, by visioning what appears a veritable paradise on earth—a grove of olives and assorted fruit trees, particularly peaches, pears, and apples, as well as a sunny vineyard. The water flowing through these gardens and which is used for irrigation comes down from the Cañada de los Verdugos. Julio Verdugo was the creator of these charming gardens.*

Upon our arrival we were greeted by the inmates with the warmest hospitality. A child on horseback—Californians are trained to ride from infancy—brought us a chair while a small boy without reins or saddle galloped by on a sorrel horse. After we were seated together with these brown, half-Indian faces under a pear tree heavy with fruit, a man brought out two knives and served us splendid watermelons. These were genuinely refreshing on a hot day. The frank hospitality with which this was offered put us quite at our ease and left the impression that, under these bronze-

This illustration of Piedra Gorda by Austrian Archduke Ludwig Louis Salvator appeared in his travel memoir *Flowers from the Golden Land. Published by the Auto Club of Southern California.*

colored countenances, Spanish blood surged. After describing what fine products were raised in their gardens, and how they were marketed in Los Angeles—they also raise apples to dry—they spoke wistfully of life in the past and of the days when there was great freedom. They live quite simply and have only three small wooden houses.

Having left this delightful spot, a valley was reached where directly ahead rose the mysterious Piedra Gorda, the goal of our journey. At the right is the Ciénega del Garvanza [at York and Eagle Rock Boulevards], *a small green swamp with clumps of bunch-grass and at the bottom, Sacate de Matico, which never dries out. From here we emerged on a plain where enormous herds of sheep, guarded by strong, fat, shaggy dogs, pastured. Nearby is the entrance into the Canyon of Piedra Gorda, a wilderness of luxuriant vegetation that forms an almost impenetrable thicket, often the haunt of wild beasts. The Piedra Gorda, towering above, is an imposing rock of granite conglomerates on one side with exposed parallel strata having two sharply defined hollows in which swallows have built their nests. It was also used at one time by the Indians as a natural bulwark, a rock fortress. Since, from this point, a fine view off across the horizon as far as Los Angeles may be had, this spot was an excellent location from which to observe the movements of the first settlers.*

Benjamin Dreyfus

As a result of the partition of the rancho, Benjamin Dreyfus became the owner of much of what would become Glendale and the city of Eagle Rock. Henry Welcome noted:

Benjamin Dreyfus was German born. He came from Europe to San Francisco in the early 1850's. By 1857 he was already a successful businessman in the Bay City. A friend and business associate of Dreyfus, August Langenberger, moved to what was soon to be known as the Anaheim Colony and with financial help from Dreyfus opened the first general store in August 1857. The Los Angeles Vineyard Society, an organization composed of 50 San Francisco German immigrants, had, at about the same time, purchased the area.

In 1883, the *Los Angeles Herald* reported:

When, in 1857, [Dreyfus] *made his appearance in Anaheim, he was by no means well appointed in the goods of this world. Partaking of the prosperity of the place, he has gone steadily forward until he is the head of one of the*

> *largest wine concerns in the United States, the famous Eagle Wine Vaults of B. Dreyfus & Co. reaching from 630 to 842 Brannan Street, San Francisco, with a branch house at No. 45 Broadway, New York.*

Continuing, the *Herald* noted of Dreyfus's advanced ideas and ambitions for wine production in the Los Angeles area:

> *Mr. Dreyfus, for instance, has set out considerable vineyards in the Riesling, the Zinfandel, the Burger, the Black Hamburg and the Queen Victoria. He has forever set at rest the question as to whether or not Los Angeles County can make a good claret. The experienced taster of the Eagle Wine Vaults has written him that the Zinfandel made from the Anaheim vines is the finest that has ever reached San Francisco. The Riesling, which may be quaffed by the favored visitor to Mr. Dreyfus's wine cellars even surpasses, in its delicate bouquet, the product of the vines of Sonoma.*

Although it is possible that he thought of planting his new acreage in Eagle Rock, mostly south-facing slopes, as vineyards, it appears Dreyfus found that selling his land for development would be far more profitable than farming. Welcome wrote of the sale:

> *For a number of years Dreyfus rented the land to graze stock, mainly sheep. He sold his undeveloped property to C.H. Watts, M.E. Hodgekins, E.T. Wright and M.L. Wicks on March 24, 1883, for $50,000. He retained the mineral and coal rights. For many years as the land was subdivided, the Dreyfus family collected 11¢ per square foot to clear this cloud from the title. When the widow died in 1912, the estate had received nearly $75,000 tribute to clear these many titles. Bank of America closed the final accounting to the family with a check for $140 dollars in 1937, bringing the grand total of nearly $77,000 over half again as much as the original sale Dreyfus made.*

The part of the rancho adjacent to the Arroyo Seco was deeded to Prudent Beaudry.

THE BEAUDRY BROTHERS AND THE CAMPBELL-JOHNSTONS

San Rafael historian Donald Crocker described Prudent Beaudry:

> *Beaudry was of French Canadian ancestry and was mayor of Los Angeles from 1874–76. Beaudry lost four of the five fortunes he amassed and was one of the first to start leveling off and subdividing the hills in downtown Los Angeles. He also pioneered water works and methods of making water available to hillside homesites. Prudent Beaudry's acquisition of the Verdugo land consisted of 1702.64 acres in a square parcel, being roughly the area encompassed by Colorado Boulevard on the north, the extension of the line formed by Meridian Avenue on the south, North Figueroa on the west, and the western bluff of the Arroyo Seco on the east.*

Geography dictated the development of this area more than in the other two. The western portion, from Loleta Avenue to the hills to the east of the valley of the Rock, was naturally connected to Eagle Rock and was gradually incorporated into it. The valley surrounding Avenue 64 was accessed most easily from Garvanza and became part of greater Highland Park. The areas eastward to the arroyo and northward to the Annandale Valley connected most easily with Pasadena and were incorporated into that city shortly after the completion of the Colorado Street Bridge.

The name Annandale, which was applied to various parts of this property, is derived from the motto under the Campbell-Johnston coat of arms, which is said by Crocker to read:

> *"Within the vale of Annandale,*
> *The gentle Johnstons ride,*
> *They've been here now a thousand years,*
> *A thousand more they'll bide."*

> *Alexander Robert Campbell-Johnston was an Englishman of distinguished Scottish lineage. Alexander had seen service in the British diplomatic service and was visiting California with his wife, Frances E. Campbell-Johnston in 1883. They visited the San Rafael area and immediately purchased over 2000 acres from Beaudry and Dreyfus for agricultural and real estate development purposes, and named it the "San Rafael Ranch" (not to be*

The Church of the Angels is the most prominent remaining structure from the Campbell-Johnston Ranch. It was constructed in 1889 by Mrs. Frances E. Campbell-Johnston as a memorial to her husband. The plans were drawn by English architect Arthur Edmund Street and adapted by Ernest A. Coxhead. *Courtesy of the Church of the Angels.*

This undated photograph is of the Stewart ranch, successor to Dominguez. The ranch was located just north of La Loma Road on what is now the power line easement. The building was demolished for the construction of the "W" line trolley to the substation behind the Rock.

> *confused with the much larger land grant "Rancho San Rafael"). Mr. Campbell-Johnston entrusted the operation of the ranch to three of his ten sons, Augustine, Conway and Alexander Napier, who were then 25, 24 and 18...Alexander R. Campbell-Johnston and his wife soon returned to England but again visited the ranch in 1888 to see its progress. Shortly after their arrival Mr. Campbell-Johnston was taken ill and passed away at the ranch on January 21, 1888. The sons continued to manage the ranch and their mother accompanied their father's remains back to England for burial.*

This firsthand account of the development of this area appeared in the seventy-fifth-anniversary history of the Church of the Angels. It is unattributed but may well be by Robert H. Lindsey, foreman on the ranch. His scrapbook, now lost, provided many of the photographs in *Within the Vale of Annandale*:

> *Mr. A.R. Campbell-Johnston purchased the Dreyfus and Beaudry Tract as well as that portion of the Rancho San Pascual which lies west of the Arroyo Seco, in 1883. At that time there was also a Tract of 180 acres situated north and east of the Dreyfus Tract which he wished to purchase, as well as a small two acre tract just west of the Eagle Rock, owned by a Mexican named Dominguez. These properties were not, however, at that time for sale but were purchased later on by Mr. H.J. Stewart, a Scotchman who had spent most of his life in China but who, on coming to this country, had leased the Chino Ranch as a sheep farm. He rebuilt the house on the Dominguez property in 1884 and lived in it for several years. When he rebuilt it, it was, I believe, about the only house in the Eagle Rock Valley. It is now included together with some of the Dreyfus land and also some of the 180 acre tract, in the Huntington Land Company's Park.*
>
> *The west boundary of the Beaudry land is now known as Peyton Avenue* [Loleta Avenue] *and was named after Mr. A.W.H. Peyton who was our manager for several years. About three hundred acres of land lying east of that street was cleared and sown in wheat by us in 1884. At that time there was just south of this land a vineyard of 22 acres planted in 1880 by some Frenchmen named Jay and Begon, which provided us with grapes for our winery for many years. There was also an old Frenchman who had a bee ranch up the Eagle Rock Canyon, who used to live in a cave in the west face of the Eagle Rock, which he had to reach by means of a ladder. He had, however, caused a good deal of trouble in the neighborhood*

Grading the Eagle Rock Road in the canyon below the Rock. *This item is reproduced by the permission of the Huntington Library, San Marino, California.*

> *and was given notice to leave by Mr. Beaudry at the time that he sold his property. In 1885 we made our first subdivision in what is now known as Annandale Valley, in the center of which was located the Garvanza Spring which gave its name to the present town of Garvanza.*

Crocker added:

> *The earliest evidence that the Campbell-Johnstons had real estate subdivision of their Ranch in mind was the preparation during 1884, and the recording in 1886, of a subdivision map for 34 lots from 2½ to 19 acres in size in the "Annandale Tract," located on both sides of what is now North Figueroa Street north of Meridian Avenue.*
>
> *On May 8, 1886, Alexander R. Campbell-Johnston through power of attorney to his son, Augustine, conveyed to the Board of Supervisors of Los Angeles County a strip of land 40 feet wide "for a new road to be called the Eagle Rock Road...now known as Colorado Boulevard."*
>
> *In about 1900 there was development of the eastern portion of the Ranch lands overlooking the Arroyo along what is now South San Rafael Avenue into estate-sized lots known as "San Rafael Heights." Within*

> *ten years, there were many large beautiful mansions completed along the east side of South San Rafael Avenue and the pattern had been set for subdivision of the San Rafael area into home sites.*
>
> *Of the three Campbell-Johnston sons who resided in California and were involved in the operation of the San Rafael Ranch, Alexander Napier died in 1907 at the age of 42, Conway lost his life at age 57 in the sinking of the Lusitania in 1915, on his way to join the military service of England, and Augustine passed away in 1920 at the age of 62. With Augustine's death the farming operations on the San Rafael Ranch were wound up.*

The most significant subdivisions of the ranch, from our point of view, were Rockdale in 1886 and the Rockdale Addition in 1887, which, when added to the Watts subdivision, formed the western portion of the city of Eagle Rock. The remainder of the Campbell-Johnston land along Figueroa Street to what is now the Pasadena city line remained as county land until it was added to the city of Los Angeles in 1923 as the Annandale Addition.

ANDREW GLASSELL AND ALFRED B. CHAPMAN

We have introduced Alfred Chapman previously as the owner, briefly, of the entire Rancho San Rafael after Verdugo's bankruptcy was settled. Andrew Glassell and Chapman as partners acquired the largest portion of the rancho out of the partition. James Miller Guinn described Andrew Glassell thus:

> [Glassell] *was the fourth in direct succession to bear the name of Andrew Glassell, the first having been a worthy Scot whose son and namesake founded the family in Virginia. When seven years of age he was taken to Sumter County, Ala., where his father became a cotton planter near Livingston. At seventeen years of age he entered the University of Alabama, from which he was graduated in 1848. Then he began the study of law…and on being admitted to the bar commenced a general professional practice…*
>
> [I]*n 1852 Mr. Glassell cast his fortunes with the new state of California…he was soon appointed a deputy of the United States district attorney of California at San Francisco. His especial assignment was the trying of a large number of land cases, some of which were then pending*

before the United States land commission, appointed under act of Congress of March 3 1851, to settle the titles to lands in this state. After three years in this position he resumed private practice in San Francisco and so continued until the war, when, on account of his southern sympathies... he temporarily closed his office. With the close of the war he again took up professional labors, selecting Los Angeles as his future home and entering into partnership with Alfred B. Chapman, a friend of his boyhood...

The New York Valley area of their holdings has a curious history. Just after the partition, during the boom of the 1880s, there was considerable interest in development of this pastoral valley with one of the largest local sources of year-round water. The Southern Pacific rail line had been completed along the Los Angeles River in 1876, and the Los Angeles and San Gabriel Railroad, later incorporated in the Santa Fe mainline, came through to Garvanza in 1885. The connection to either of these was by unimproved dirt wagon roads. A new rail line was reported in the *Los Angeles Herald* on November 10, 1888:

It is authoritatively given out that the Glendale extension to Pasadena will be in operation in three months from date. Mr. John Cross has placed the $200,000 bonds needful to carry out the enterprise and it is said has already contracted for the ties, steel and rolling stock, all of which are now in course of construction in Eastern shops. The line should be a paying one from the start, for after leaving the Glendale motor road at the Boulevard Tract, it runs through a very fertile stretch of country into the Eagle Rock Valley, and so on to Pasadena. This land is not all settled up now owing to the poor facilities for transportation, but the arrival of the iron horse will soon see every foot of land occupied. The route is marked out and everything is ready for the shovels of the graders.

This road was never built. A wagon road from Pasadena across Campbell-Johnston's toll bridge in the arroyo—roughly tracing what is now Colorado Boulevard, turning south in Eagle Rock and following the valley into the Boulevard Tract (now Glassell Park)—is shown on a hand-drawn map in the records of the Campbell-Johnston's San Rafael Ranch in the Huntington Library collection.

Finally, a route from Garvanza to Eagle Rock was built. An article in the *Los Angeles Herald* on April 15, 1889, noted:

One of those exciting episodes which occasionally occur during railroad construction enlivened the Eagle Rock valley yesterday, to the disgust, however, of the residents of that place. The Garvanza, or Rogers Railroad, as it is better known, has been so often mentioned in these columns that a detailed description of it is unnecessary. A section of it, about 4½ miles in length, was built from Garvanza west into the Eagle Rock valley last spring, but was never used for more than a week, as it was claimed that the patronage was not sufficient for its support. In point of fact, it was only a "boom" road conceived by Rogers when things were at their best, and although Eagle Rock Valley is not thickly populated the inhabitants on having pointed out to them the immense advantages which were to accrue to them through the road, subsidized, it is said, the affair to the amount of $15,000. They therefore regarded the line to a certain extent as their own and although it was not in operation they jealously watched it when the

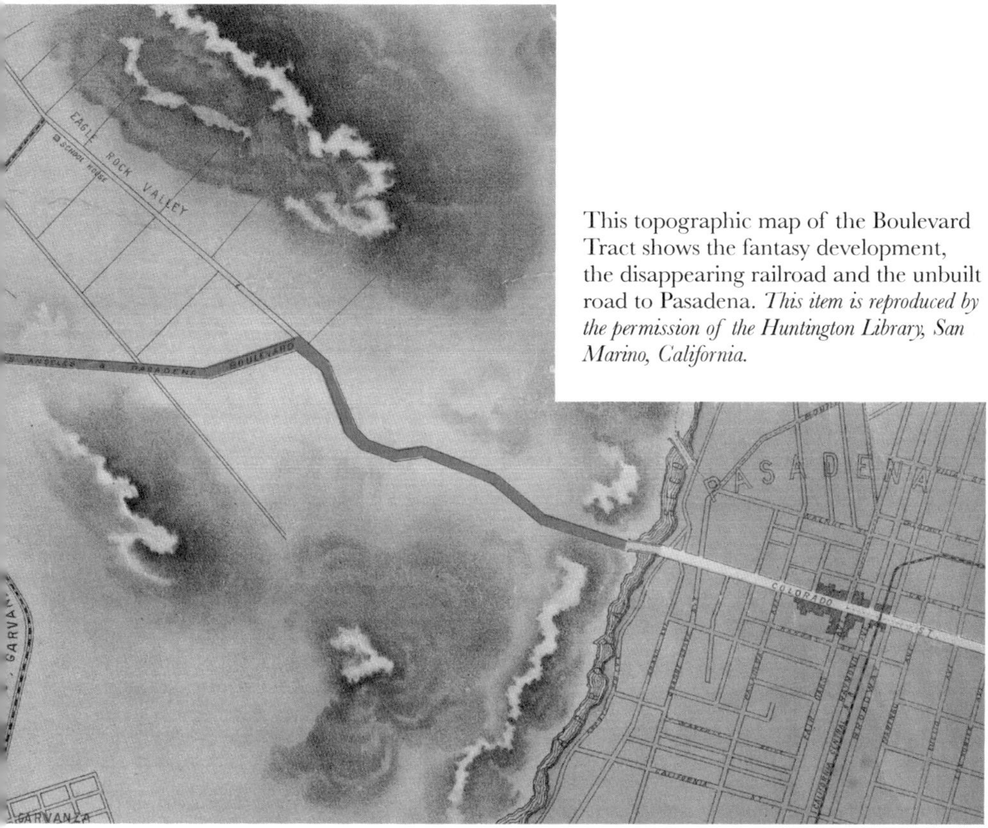

This topographic map of the Boulevard Tract shows the fantasy development, the disappearing railroad and the unbuilt road to Pasadena. *This item is reproduced by the permission of the Huntington Library, San Marino, California.*

Rogers lines, including of course the Eagle Rock branch, were transferred to the Nathan Cole syndicate. They were somewhat aroused shortly afterwards, for the rumor got about that Eagle Rock was to be boomed up again, but their hopes fell with a terrible crash when, a few weeks ago, the road passed into the hands of a company controlled by Captain John Cross, the President of the Los Angeles, Glendale and Pacific Road. The announcement was then made that the main line was to be extended into Pasadena at once, but although it was not openly declared, it was generally understood that the Eagle Rock branch had been declared useless by the company. The dwellers of the little valley determined, however, to keep their road where it was, and Captain Cross and party realizing the situation determined to bring the matter to a focus by taking up the track at once. The plan of action was, however, kept very quiet, and Contractors McCrabbe and Backman were instructed to have a force of men and teams on hand on Saturday last after nightfall, and to start in and remove the disputed branch line.

At 9 o'clock on the night appointed, 110 men and sixty teams drew into Garvanza, and at once commenced the task before them. They removed the bolts and spikes, and by daybreak yesterday were hard at work tearing up the rails and ties and freighting them into Garvanza. The residents of the Eagle Rock Valley soon got wind of what was going on, and came down in force and ordered the workmen to desist. It looked at one time as if a big row would occur, but the contractors explained that their laborers were simply acting under orders from headquarters. An endeavor was then made to get a writ of injunction, but it being Sunday this was supposed to be impossible, Capt. Cross having laid his plans to thus prevent any legal interference. There was nothing to be done, therefore, but to look on at the work of destruction, and at 7 in the evening the last wagon-load was started, and the unpleasant task of the workmen was over. Altogether about 320 tons of material were removed and freighted into Garvanza, where it now lies and will be used on the extension of the main line. The citizens, in the neighborhood affected, declare that they will not let their rights be over-ridden in such a manner, and the affair will doubtless get into the courts today.

The collapse of the land boom meant that there were no longer any customers or financing for these projects. Ownership of the Boulevard Tract seems to have reverted to Glassell. The area would await development until a syndicate, again involving Ralph Rogers, enticed Occidental College to move and centered Occidental Park on the college property. By that time, 1909, two trolley lines had been built to the area.

PART IV
FARMERS AND VILLAGERS

The first known reference to the "Eagle Rock" valley appeared in the *Los Angeles Herald* on May 11, 1883, as part of a description of the land subdivided by Watts's syndicate:

> *To the southeast and east, hills bound that beautiful valley, locally known as the Eagle Rock valley, because that celebrated rock is conspicuous at its east end, on the western slope of the Verdugo Mountains, which drop into the Arroyo Seco on the eastern slope.*

Farming the Valley

In his memoir, published in 1913 in the *Eagle Rock Sentinel*, Cromwell Galpin, an early landowner and one of the first to farm the valley, related the following:

> [V]*alley history begins about 1882, for previous to that date the Eagle Rock was only a landmark of the San Rafael Rancho, the old Spanish grant…Watts' subdivision was subdivided some more; some of the land was sold to settlers and modern history began. By January 1, 1883, a Mr. Green had built a house and planted some trees on the hill north of*

The renamed Eagle Rock looms above the valley below. When the angle of the sun is right, caves throw an eagle-shaped shadow. This, the earliest known photo, was taken in 1888 by a Kodak camera, and the photo was sent to the Eagle Rock Chamber of Commerce in 1924 by a man in Palo Alto. It ended up in the collection of Mrs. C.W. Young. *Courtesy of the Louanna Clark, Emma Young Collection.*

Cromwell Galpin built this home for his family. He grew onions in the farmland to the east prior to subdividing "Shallot Terrace" in 1911. Pelican Rock is at the right. *Photograph by Rollin McNitt.*

> *the present terminus of the Eagle Rock car line* [Colorado Boulevard at Townsend Avenue]. *It was the only house in the valley...In 1883 and 1884 more settlers came in and within the next two years the valley began to assume the half-settled appearance characteristic of the region surrounding Los Angeles. All the land from the present southern city limits to Colorado Street* [Colorado Boulevard], *between Central Avenue* [Eagle Rock Boulevard] *and the hills to the west; all the land north of Colorado Street, and most of that lying east of Central Avenue, had been bought by men who intended to make a living by farming. Plowing began with the late coming of rain in 1884, and tree planting followed rapidly.*

Born in Eagle, Wisconsin, in 1853, Galpin moved with his family to Appleton, where his father started a hardware business. Cromwell attended Lawrence University there. He received a law degree from the University of Michigan in 1875. He married Julia Wood, with whom he had three children. They moved to Saginaw, where he began a law practice, but he soon become editor of the *Evening News* of Saginaw. According to John Steven McGroarty, "After his arrival in California in 1883, Galpin was on a hunting trip with friends in Eagle Rock valley, impressed with the area, he soon purchased land to try farming." After Eagle Rock became a city, he was elected to the city board of trustees, serving until 1922, and was the mayor of Eagle Rock from 1914 to 1916.

A much younger contemporary of Galpin's, Elena Frackelton Murdock, came to Eagle Rock at the age of six with her parents, John and Katherine Frackelton. She compiled a family album of photos, with notes highlighting her memories of growing up on the family farm. While Galpin's writings focus on the business of farming the valley, Murdock's words show the wonder of a schoolgirl on a new adventure:

> *I caught my first sight of Eagle Rock in October 1886. We had hired a horse and buggy in East Los Angeles and driven to Eagle Rock for dinner with the Brierley family. We had come from Rhode Island, due to mother's ill health, to the valley, which was surrounded by greasewood covered mountains. After dinner, father decided to buy seven acres and farm it. He had been an iron molder and knew nothing of farming, but friendly neighbors advised and helped. We had to remove the greasewood and we built a small house on the hill. We moved in (during a storm) before it was complete.*

They moved in on February 4, 1887. Their second family home still stands on Frackelton Place. Murdock attended, and then taught, in Eagle Rock's first school when it still had only two rooms. In 1910, she married Ray Murdock, and they had three children. For many years, she was a teacher and principal in Los Angeles schools. She lived in Eagle Rock for eighty-seven years.

BEAUTIFUL BUT REMOTE

Murdock continued:

> *Wild flowers grew abundantly in the vacant fields with many yuccas on the mountains. Among the flowers were Four O' Clocks, Shooting Stars, Poppies, Forget-Me-Nots (white), Blue Grass, Yellow Violets, Maiden Hair Ferns, Hair Bells (blue), Chocolate Lilies, Blue Bells, Gold backed Ferns, which when pressed on back of our hands, left a lovely gold impression.*
>
> *Gopher snakes, small garter snakes, rattlers, red racers and Mexican Adders were seen here in early days…No one killed gopher snakes. They were never known to bite people and kept the gophers down.*
>
> *All hen houses had to be built with no small openings; otherwise skunks got in and killed the chickens on the roosts. Many coyotes lived in the mountains and on moonlight nights we would hear them yipping and barking in great numbers. Before we were married, we were sitting in a hammock in the back yard, one evening, and two coyotes trotted by us, not thirty feet away.*
>
> *On the Percy Schumacher ranch, near Hill Drive were many quail. He used to feed them and never allowed any shooting on the ranch. If there was a dead animal in the mountains or canyons, the buzzards would gather and wheel in the sky by the dozen…Before a big storm, many sea gulls flew here from the ocean and would land where the farmers were plowing. Flocks of wild geese flew from north to south. Later they flew north in big Vs with a leader guiding them and the birds honking. As the years passed, we saw fewer of the geese…Before trees grew high enough to obstruct the view, we could see river fog rising from Los Angeles River. Looking toward Los Feliz, we could plainly see the "Sleeping Giant" lying along the tops of the Los Feliz mountains. He is still there, but not seen as plainly. There were very*

Elena Frackelton Murdock is seen here in a field of wildflowers. *Courtesy of the Elena Frackelton Murdock family.*

few large trees then. One of the largest was the big oak tree near Hill Drive and the Lemon Grove. It was immense in 1886, and beautiful, until cut down...in 1954.

Standing on our hill, when we shouted, echoes came from all directions in the north valley. Early, near dawn, some roosters would crow. Answering crows came from ranches all over the Valley. Eagle Rock was so quiet that we could clearly hear the bell from the Church of the Angels, and also the bass drum when the Salvation Army band played over in Pasadena, and the trains going over the Arroyo bridge in Highland Park.

Father went back to his trade in a foundry in Los Angeles, when money was needed for food, trees to be planted, horse and cow feed, taxes and wells, which were always caving in. He drove seven miles each way with a horse and two-wheeled cart. There was no bridge across the arroyo near Ave. 35, where he crossed it, and he had to ford the stream. During storms he could not cross and could not be home until after the storm.

There were only two east–west streets, Old County Road [Colorado Boulevard] *and Sycamore* [Yosemite Drive]. *The main north–south street was called Central* [Eagle Rock Boulevard]. *There was also a short street north from County Road to the Brierley and Frackelton homes called Peyton Ave.* [Loleta Avenue] *No doctors here, so Mrs. Brierley helped as midwife when a new baby was born.*

The nearest doctor was Dr. Harlan Shoemaker who lived on the east side. To get him, some one had to drive or ride horseback to his home. A spider bit my father, and Dr. Shoemaker said "Oh, my poor brother. I hate to see you so sick."

In the middle 1880's, the early settlers had to get their mail from Pasadena, Verdugo or East Los Angeles Station A. Later the East Los Angeles mail was sent to Garvanza...In the early 1900's Free Rural Delivery was given us. Mr. & Mrs. Lee Adams delivered for many years by horse & buggy, not to houses, boxes were put on the edges of properties by the road.

Cromwell Galpin recounted:

Building supplies and farming implements of course had to be brought from Los Angeles, and the roads were a horror when the rains came. Colorado Avenue had been handed down from mission days as the stage line from San Bernardino to Santa Barbara. Central Avenue was so marked on the map of Watts' subdivision; but it stopped at about the southern city limits.

> [When the traveler] *went farther afoot, he took his choice of a route across or around the hills, across a morass if he turned to the right, and into the water if he went ahead; he then turned to the left, went farther and fared worse; for he got into bottomless and almost boundless mud over in what is now a very pleasant part of New York Valley. But the settler went to town, and he went numerously, and with a prayer or a swear word, according to his early training or later acquired habits, he got back again; sometimes with a load and sometimes with part of a load of seed barley or such bundles of trees as ready cash or full stretched credit enabled him to obtain.*

Murdock recalled attempts to improve access:

> *During the boom in the late 80's a railroad was built from Townsend Avenue to Garvanza. It was very odd. The first day it came we went down and decorated it with roses and went for the ride. It did not last long, as it didn't take us any place we wanted to go. Early one Sunday morning we heard clanging. A big crowd of workmen was digging up the tracks. Good-by railroad.*
>
> *Before the* [Los Angeles] *railway in 1906, there was an Eagle Rock Stage to Avenue 60 in Highland Park. It was a three-seated surrey with two horses, driven by Mrs. James Kincheloe's brother.*

Throughout the 1880s, the land that Watts and his syndicate put on the market changed hands several hundred times. Many bought the land for pure speculation, others like Galpin speculated but also grew produce and some, like John Frackelton, farmed the land to support their families. For many, like the Whites, farming was a community enterprise.

Galpin described how commercial farmers used their properties:

> *A Mr. Brown had forty acres now embraced in Artesian Heights and Almond Heights tracts, and he had planted walnuts on the flat grounds and apricots on the hillside; Myers to the north planted apricots on the flat; and Galpin had apples and apricots on all the flat ground of the Shallot Terrace Tract, and apricots halfway up the hill and peaches as high as plowing was practicable. Fish had apricots and apples on large portion of the Hamilton Tract; Woolley owned all the land from Sycamore Avenue to Colorado Avenue, and put in a large number of trees, chiefly apricots, and also put in five or ten acres of pears on what the map shows as the Adams Tract. Parker and Green set out many apricots and peaches, and a small*

Above: The horse-drawn bus route ran from Townsend and Colorado, over the hill into the valley of the rock, over the stream and up the hill to Avenue 60 in Garvanza in the early 1900s. Otto Owen was the driver. In front are Bob and Bill Broxholme. In the second seat is Mrs. R.V. Frackelton. In the third are Charlie Broxholme and Mabel Myers. *Courtesy of the Elena Frackelton Murdock family.*

Opposite, top: John Frackelton, plowing. *Courtesy of the Elena Frackelton Murdock family.*

Opposite, bottom: The Whites and their neighbors are planting onions. William White is the second from the left. The Whitney girls are setting out the onions. Lottie White holds her dog at the right. The ranch buildings are in the middle distance. *Courtesy of the Elena Frackelton Murdock family.*

Top: The modest homestead of the Townsend family is depicted in 1887. *Courtesy of the Elena Frackelton Murdock family.*

Bottom: The Byron Myers home was built in the fashionable Victorian style. It still stands at the southern end of Vincent Avenue. *Courtesy of the Elena Frackelton Murdock family.*

number of orange trees. The low ground in the center of the valley was largely planted to barley.

Murdock recalled:

In the eastern end was the home of an old English couple named Townsend. Townsend Avenue is named for them, and is the only street with the original name.

When we moved to Eagle Rock, Feb. 4, 1887 nineteen families were living here. Eighteen people were under eighteen years old. At the end of the 1880's, eight new families had moved in. In the early 1890's sixteen more, including the Myers, Grandma Myers, Byron, Emmet, Mahlon, Leander, Charlie, Callie, Alice, Nettie, and Lola. After the middle 1890's, the new families began to move in thick and fast.

LIFE ON THE FARM

Murdock wrote:

When Allie Parker and Will Frackelton were married, they put down a wood floor, pitched a tent over it, and lived under the Oak, until their house was built. When houses were first built many families did not have money to properly finish the inside. Yards of unbleached muslin were used for sidewalls and ceilings. When the wind blew, we could get seasick, watching the ceilings billow. Later, the inside was finished in wood or plaster. The muslin was washed and made into scratchy sheets and pillowcases.

[Murdock remembered] *visiting in a kitchen, seeing one of the front stove lids off, and a long, thick branch, poked in the fire. As the wood burned down, it was pushed in further. Mrs. Brierley's wood stove had a big water tank built into the back of the stove. When fire was burning, water was always hot. When there was a surplus of skim milk, our mothers washed the linoleum with it. Made it nice and shining, just like wax. To scour pans and kettles we used ashes from the wood and coal stove.*

There was one part of farm life that my mother disliked. The house, barn and chicken yard were on top of a red clayey hill. The small chicks would scratch the clay soil and it would stick to their feet and form clay balls on their toes. She would get a pan of warm water, soak their feet and break off the hard balls so they could walk and scratch for food again. When the lining of the fire box in the wood stove cracked and fell out, all that had to be done was to go out on the hill, get some of the red dirt, add water, and line the fire box. The red soil made a fine fire clay that lasted for a long time.

Children in those days made money cutting fruit, picking peas, picking up prunes, planting little onion plants. Mr. Parker would spread a tarp under a big prune tree. The children would lie on it, face down. The men shook the trees. After the pelting prunes fell, children got paid so much a bucket to pick them up. Dried peaches sold better if peeled before drying. Some were hand peeled; we had a glorified eggbeater machine to peel with. A prong out front held pit & knives on wheel peeled. Then they had to be cut & placed on trays. It was a long, tedious job.

On a night when a "cold snap" was expected, preparations were started the night before. Bales of hay were put on the sled. About three o'clock in the morning, the family got up, dressed warmly, hitched the horse to the sled and went to the "Winter Tomato" patch. Mother drove, a small child held a lantern, and father covered the tomato vines with hay. With good luck, the tomatoes were saved to ship to the East.

Mr. Parker would go to Pasadena and get boxes and tubs of oranges. He would put them in his barn and let all the neighborhood children come and eat them at any time, but they must save all the seeds. These he planted, and when they grew to small trees, he sold them to nurserymen, who budded them to good varieties. I often wonder, when eating our oranges now, if they are descendants of some of the seeds we saved.

In 1886 Mr. Galpin let school be held in his barn for the first 6 week term. The first teacher was Miss Hutchins, who boarded with the Greens, one mile away. The barn had a partition in the middle, the school on one side, the animals on the other.

Eagle Rock's first schoolhouse was built in 1887 by community volunteers on land donated by Cromwell Galpin south of Colorado Boulevard and east of Caspar Avenue. Murdock continued:

About seven years after the schoolhouse was built, the Trustees took pity on the children who had to eat in the sun. They had an "Eating House" built: No sides, a roof, and a long table and benches. In the middle, up through the roof, was a large flagpole. We had to stand on the table to raise the flag.

In this 1888 student body photograph, the teacher, shown at rear, is Will Frackelton. Elena Frackelton, his niece, is fifth from the left in front. *Courtesy of the Elena Frackelton Murdock family.*

Miss King, the teacher, had my mother make the first flag flown over an Eagle Rock School. Each star was carefully hand sewn to the flag. The eating house and flag pole raising was on Columbus Day, 1892, 400 years after his discovery of America.

Christmas was always celebrated in the schoolhouse. Mothers met and made red tarlatan stockings, edged with buttonholed stitching, and filled them with candy bought in Well's Candy Store in Los Angeles, and with nuts and popcorn. A large cypress tree was cut and set up in the school building and popcorn strings, candles, and gifts hung on it. Santa arrived in a homemade red suit with a pillow in his middle.

Many times the children walked over to the Church of the Angels, especially on Easter Sunday. Services were always in the daytime, as there were no lighting arrangements. We always tried to get a pew where we could look back of the Pipe Organ and watch the boy pump it by hand. Where the Security Bank [Chase Bank] *is now was a hill. Every year the camp meeting in the big tent was held there, and we all "Got Religion" year after year.*

The first gatherings took place at the School; Church, Sunday school, W.C.T.U., Improvement Association, Sewing Bees, Reading Club. Instead of Prayer Meeting in the middle of the week, some neighbors gathered and sang Gospel Hymns. If it was a "Dry Year" and rain was badly needed, the song most often sung was "Showers of Blessing"...

Every summer we all went to Long Beach, and the women and children spent a few weeks or a month. We pitched tents in the sand and carried water from a nearby house. The party gathered at three a.m., hitched horses to already packed wagons and began the trip. We stopped at the Willows for lunch, and covered the 33 miles by nightfall. The worst was getting through the sand to the beach. Everyone pushed and loads were lightened. The Long Beach camping trips lasted until 1896 when Frank Sherman and Harry Dickerson drowned in the rip tide.

Some families came here to be together. Ruth Orchard married Philip W. Parker in Illinois. The Parkers were followed by Ruth's mother, Ann Orchard, along with Ruth's two sisters and their husbands, Frances Jane and James Brierley and Mary Ann and James Hickson.

The Parkers named their home Rosemont Villa for the prize roses, grown for sale, surrounding it. The family allowed the community to use the lower portion of their land as a park and their pond as a swimming hole. P.W. Parker organized the Eagle Rock School District and was trustee from Eagle Rock of the Union High School District.

United Church historian Medora Swinnerton recounted:

In 1884 there being no church within driving distance, and feeling the need of Christian Education for the children, Mrs. P.W. Parker started a Sunday School in her home. In 1886 when the first school was built, the Sunday School moved into the school house, and there the first church services were held. The congregation, being of all denominations, named it Union Church.

Opposite, top: The Shakespeare Club met at the home of Mahlon Myers. Mrs. Broxholme, Frackelton, Myers, Knighttinger and Parker brought culture and style to their new homes. *Courtesy of the Elena Frackelton Murdock family.*

Opposite, bottom: James and Mary Hickson built their home, Esperanza, in 1888 on their large farm, which extended from the ridgeline to Colorado Boulevard. The house remains on Mount Royal Drive today. *Courtesy of the Elena Frackelton Murdock family.*

In front of Rosemont, standing (left to right), are Mrs. Brierly and her child, Mrs. Ruth Parker and P.W. Parker. Grandma Ann Orchard and an unknown woman are seated on the rock wall. The descendants of Mrs. Orchard would develop large portions of Eagle Rock. *Courtesy of the Elena Frackelton Murdock family.*

Hearing of a minister who lived in Hollywood, and served a church there in the morning, Mr. Parker asked him to come to Eagle Rock in the afternoon. So Reverend Elijah Cash, a Congregational minister, became the first pastor of Union Church. Mrs. Cash was State President of the W.C.T.U. and organized a chapter in Eagle Rock. Mr. Parker was the first Deacon and Sunday School Superintendent. In 1887 the Church was chartered as "The Church of Christ, Congregational."

Because roads were poor, and horse and buggy driving was slow, the time of arrival of Rev. Cash was very uncertain. The church members came with picnic baskets for lunch. A row of tall eucalyptus trees along Eagle Rock Road, now Colorado St., made good hitching posts for the horses. Tables

The "Little Brown Church in the Vale" was the first civic building that faced Colorado Boulevard. *Courtesy of the Elena Frackelton Murdock family.*

were set up using saw horses and planks, and all shared in the first Church Dinners. Church service started when the minister arrived. If he happened to be late or the sermon long, and darkness came, the people lighted their lanterns and the bobbing lights, like fire flies, could be seen going across the fields to their homes. Rev. Cash always stayed over night with a member of the church. There was considerable rivalry among the women as to whose turn it was to entertain. Mrs. Cash always accompanied her husband. In those days money was scarce and the minister was often paid in produce from the hillside farms and orchards.

By 1898 the congregation had outgrown the school building, and plans were made for building the first little church at Castle and Eagle Rock

> *Road, now Caspar and Colorado. By gifts of material, labor and money, the "Little Brown Church in the Vale" was erected. For many years this was the social center of the valley.*

With a population at the end of the eighteenth century of only one hundred people, many of the first settlers married, including Viola Knowles and Milton Brown, Allie Parker and William Frackelton, Nellie Binkley and Charlie Brierley, Allie Myers and Arthur Parker, Tilly Sherman and Ray Wickerd and Kate Isbel and Will Prosser.

RAINWATER

The editor of the *Eagle Rock Sentinel* quizzed Cromwell Galpin in 1911:

> *Knowledge is of two kinds—we know a thing ourselves, or we know where to get the information. Many theories have been advanced and many statements made regarding the source and quantity of Eagle Rock's water supply in the past and future. Not knowing anything about the real facts ourselves, and having a desire only to get the conditions before our readers, we asked Mr. Cromwell Galpin to give us some facts and figures.*
>
> *Eagle Rock Valley began to attract settlers in 1883, but a year or two earlier attempts to obtain artesian water had been made by the late Andrew Glassell. One well, with six-inch casing, was put down in the lowest portion of the valley, a little east and a little south of the place where the present car line intersects the city line* [Eagle Rock Boulevard and Langdale Avenue]. *The pipe stood a couple of feet above ground and water, roughly estimated at six miners' inches, ran over the top of the pipe, and, if it is not running yet, it was a few months ago. That well was a decided success and was accepted by some purchasers of land as good proof of the existence of the inexhaustible underground river. Two other wells were put down about the same time north of the hill in the center of the valley, one not far from the present corner of Stanley Avenue* [Chickasaw Avenue] *and Pearl Street* [Shearin Avenue] *and the other between Highlands* [Highland View Avenue] *and Kenilworth* [Hermosa] *Avenues. Both wells flowed, but in measure so small as to cause their abandonment.*

The rainfall was but nine inches in 1885, but the forty inches of the previous year was still draining down the hills and the lower ground was kept wet, and the trees grew beautifully. Harvest time fulfilled the promise of spring, and until 1889 fruit crops were good, considering the age of the trees.

In October, 1889, it began to rain, and it kept on until nearly seven inches had fallen; it also kept on raining a lot more in the months following, until in May 1890, the local rain gauge indicated forty-two inches and Eagle Rock valley was afloat, though the "highest mountains" still poked their heads above the flood.

When the water receded, all the apples, apricots and peaches and Brown's walnuts had been drowned; in the course of time to be cut up for fuel wherewith the Eagle Rock farmer was just moderately glad to eke out a substitute for money he might have made by farming. The whole stretch of flat ground from Park [Fair Park] *Avenue to the city limits, and west of Central* [Eagle Rock Boulevard] *was a huge morass that grew up immediately to willows, or, where the water was still too deep, to cattails or tules. The willows grew thirty feet high in a year, and were so close together as to make the fight for existence a struggle for standing room. Then the willows were hewed with axes and snagged at with scythes and wallowed around with plows until a ditch had been cut from Park Avenue to below the city limits, and the surplus water drained off. Then tomatoes were planted, and though the price was but $7 a ton, the Eagle Rocker who failed to clean up $300 an acre on "tomats" admitted that his crop was rather a failure.*

The rainfall in 1893 was almost 27 inches, since which time no year's precipitation has reached twenty inches. As the soil grew a little drier, the low ground from Adams Avenue [Addison Way] *to the city limits, west of Central, was put into alfalfa, and yielded tremendous crops for some years, the output declining with lessened rainfall and better drainage, until about the first of this century, the last of it was plowed up.*

But long before the beginning of the new century the farmers of the valley had begun to express a very anxious interest, not in the water supply, but the lack of it. Trees showed signs of drought and crops were small. Eagle Rockers began freely to admit that artificial irrigation must be resorted to.

P.W. Parker was the enterprising pioneer to take the irrigation bull by the horns, and he did not win the first bout of the wrestle. In company with two or three others Mr. Parker had a well dug south of Colorado Avenue, not far from Virginia Avenue [Vincent Avenue] *finding what seemed to be an ample supply of water. Pumping of irrigation water had not been reduced to a science in those days, but a young steam engine was purchased, some pipe and*

The fields of the Gates strawberry ranch were tended by Chinese crews brought in to work the fruit. Then, as now, strawberries were a labor-intensive crop. Eagle Rock Boulevard and the hills to the west can be seen behind the workers. *Courtesy of the Elena Frackelton Murdock family.*

pump provided, and a man hired to run the plant. Also the farmers devoted themselves intermittently to the hauling of coal from town and "snaking" of wood down from the mountains. They got some water, but the expense of labor and material was painfully in excess of the total value of crops produced, and the plant was dismantled. Then followed the driving of tunnels into the mountains, many of which yielded water for domestic purposes until the season happened to be rather dry. None ever proved of value for irrigating.

Meantime the internal combustion engine had got out of swaddling clothes and grown to be a very promising adolescent. Gasoline engines, as compared with steam apparatus were cheap, effective and easily run. The dug well gave way to the bored well, and though some of the bored wells proved to be "dry holes," most of the men who searched for water with a drilling outfit found it before they quit the search.

Barley and oats gave way largely to garden truck and tomatoes, yielded to small fruits and berries. By 1902 the valley had gained some reputation

> *as the place of production of superior strawberries, and a year or two later the larger portion of the flat ground in the valley was devoted to the crop. The Gates tract, at the corner of Central* [Eagle Rock Boulevard] *and Sycamore* [Yosemite Drive], *twenty acres with two twelve inch wells and a thirty horse-power engine to supply water, being the largest field and perhaps the best, though Adams, White, Lucas, the three Dickensons, and several others had well cared for fields of good size.*
>
> *Berry farming was fairly remunerative until the Japanese went into it rather heavily particularly in the Gardena, Tropico and Burbank regions. Prices went down and Eagle Rock growers plowed up the berries and planted more "truck," especially onions and lettuce-that is all except Mr. Gates.*
>
> *In 1891 the United States Geological Survey made a topographical survey of the region, followed by a careful examination of the water supply, the investigation lasting until 1905 and the results published, with maps, in 1907...the conclusion was reached and expressed without hesitation or qualification that the water supply of the Pasadena Quadrangle, of which Eagle Rock forms the western central portion, depends absolutely and entirely on the rainfall.*

Adding to water concerns, there was continual difficulty transporting produce to town. The outlying farmers faced additional license fees if they arrived late to the produce market. They formed the Eagle Rock Improvement Association, headed by P.W. Parker, E.D. Goode and, later, James A. Gates. With groups in Glendale, they petitioned for equal access; they even considered opening a second market outside of downtown.

PART V
DREAMERS AND SCHEMERS

A New Hometown

Eagle Rock continued to attract newcomers. In 1961, Eleanor Zimmerman interviewed Beth Ellenwood Newhan, Edith Eckert and May M. Blumer for her *Eagle Rock Sentinel* series on the area's pioneers. Although the articles were based on interviews, they were written in the third person.

Lily Beth Newhan was the daughter of William H. Ellenwood and Virginia Ellenwood. William was born in Henry County, Illinois, in 1840. After marrying Virginia Cole, he moved to Adams County, Iowa. Between 1864 and 1888, they had sixteen children, thirteen of which lived to adulthood. They fled to California in 1900, leaving everything behind, including newly purchased dishes and silverware, after a neighbor's windmill and cowshed were dumped by a cyclone into their cow field. In 1906, Beth Ellenwood married Charles Newhan.

> *For the first two years* [the Ellenwoods] *settled in Pomona, but found water scarce there and came to Eagle Rock where springs were plentiful. They purchased 32½ acres...the area of present day Ellenwood Drive from Colorado Boulevard to the top of the hills. The family home was on the northeast corner of Hill and Ellenwood. Their acreage was planted with walnuts and Kelsey plums. Along with everyone else in the valley, they kept a horse and cow. The lot was still covered with tomato plants. They*

Country gentleman William Ellenwood is depicted in front of his new family home at Hill and Ellenwood Drives. He subdivided his land following its contours, using a unique oval plan. *Courtesy of Donna Zinser.*

> *had to wait while the water mains were installed from the Blumer's. At first they had only a garage house with a plank for a drain board, and only cold water and no bathtub. Around 1913 they sold the knoll of their ranch to the Bessolos, who built the beautiful home north of Colorado, and just west of the present day Ellenwood Drive.*
>
> *...In those days walking was the accepted mode of transportation in Eagle Rock. The Ellenwoods walked to and from church in Glendale. They would often bring friends home with them, hike to the Eagle Rock, and then walk them back to Glendale.*

Any Eagle Rock student who wished to go to high school walked to Glendale, first to St. Hilda's and then, after 1904, to the new Union High School near Brand Boulevard.

> *Mrs. Newhan also remembers her interest in the dances at the Gates Ranch. She would have loved to go with her brother, but their father disapproved, and they respected his wishes, although they did consider disobeying. Today* [October 5, 1961] *Mrs. Newhan lives in a trailer in the Eagle Rock*

Eagle Rockers gathered at this barbeque at St. Hilda's, once the Glendale Hotel. It had become an Episcopal girls' school and then became the Union High School for the area. It later housed the Glendale Sanitarium. *Courtesy of the Elena Frackelton Murdock family.*

Fred and Edith Eckert are depicted on the porch of their home, which was built on a lot in the newly subdivided "Gates Tract." *Courtesy of Edith Eckert.*

Springs Park. Nearby is a spring, which ran to Central Avenue [Eagle Rock Boulevard] *where watercress grew by the side of the road. Water still runs constantly along the side of Chickasaw to the storm drain.*

Edith Eckert arrived in Eagle Rock on July 4, 1887, to join her husband, Fred. She came by train, the first time she had ever traveled alone:

The decision to leave their Wallkill, New York home came when Mr. Eckert was advised to seek a more temperate climate for his health. He had to give up a profitable position with a man named Borden, who had just "invented" condensed milk…

So it must have been with some nostalgia that Mrs. Eckert left her little home community and headed west for the rough frontier of "Eagle Rock," where one had to use a horse and buggy to get to Highland Park and mail was delivered at a place called Tropico (near Glendale).

Eckert went to work for a man by the name of Gates who owned a huge strawberry ranch. Mrs. Eckert recalls the early morning scene on the ranch when a horse drawn wagon traveling all the way from Los Angeles arrived with a cargo of 75 Chinese who worked the strawberry fields [see photo on page 80].

In 1906 Eckert built the home where Mrs. Eckert still lives, located on Sycamore Street [Yosemite Drive]. *Because the Eckerts had the only telephone for miles around, "visitors" who dropped in to use the phone were legion. At first the home was lighted with ornate kerosene lamps but the progressive Eckerts were one of the first families to install electric lighting.*

Mrs. Eckert helped found "The Friendly Club," a group of ladies who boasted a treasury of $5.60 and each one "bought" her own chair, those who were well off bought two or three. The Friendly Club prospered handsomely, and later changed its name to the Twentieth Century Club, one of the largest and most impressive women's clubs in Southern California. Mrs. Eckert is now [1961] *the only living member of that first "Friendly" group and has served the club in many capacities.*

Fred Eckert later became supervisor of the Eagle Rock Water Company and was an assistant city marshal in Eagle Rock. May Blumer recalled to Mrs. Zimmerman how she first came to visit:

A tourist from Chicago in the Spring of 1906, I met Mabel Myers whose parents lived on a ranch in the Eagle Rock Valley. The women of the Valley were having a social and educational club meeting at her mother's home and Mabel was going out to help serve luncheon and enticed me to go along and help. There were no streetcars here then, but she had a bicycle parked back of a drug store on Pasadena Avenue [Figueroa Street] *so we took the streetcar from my aunt's place in L.A. to that point, then in our full and long skirted white dresses with many lace petticoats and high white shoes, with lisle stockings and good sized leghorn hats, we set out—I on the handle bars. All went well for the civilized part of the ride along Pasadena Ave. but when we cut down on the dirt road there were many rocks and rills and the hillside seemed very steep, we went over the handle bars many times, with bike and all rolling into ditches on the way. But it was dry dirt, and we carefully brushed ourselves off and went on, arriving not too late. (We were taken back later in a "Buckboard" drawn by a tired gray-white horse.) The ladies had set up tables with blue and white checked cloths for about two dozen guests, and there I met some of the members who have been loyal over the years to those early club days spent together.*

LET'S CUT IT UP AND SELL IT

While Newhan, Eckert and Blumer enjoyed the small community of Eagle Rock at the turn of the twentieth century, many old landowners and entrepreneurial newcomers saw Eagle Rock as a potential suburb of the growing city of Los Angeles. A few stand out, particularly James A. Gates, Godfrey Edwards and James Ferdon.

In 1901, James Gates purchased about forty acres of land from the Sherman and Lamb families in the area between Eagle Rock Boulevard and Maywood Avenue and Yosemite Drive and Chickasaw Avenue. He planted strawberries and participated in the Berry Growers Association, with growers in Glendale and Tropico. Gates Hall, built in about 1903, became the social center of the valley. Mrs. Mary Gates, a founding member of the Women's Club, hosted many early meetings in her home. Dances were held that almost everyone attended. The music was provided by a player piano that everyone took turns pumping. Folks returned home across the fields by lamp or moonlight.

Gates continued to purchase additional acreage, including the area on the north east side of Colorado Boulevard and Caspar Avenue, where he built Symphony Hall, Eagle Rock's first two-story commercial building. Gates

The Gates family—James K., Mrs. Gates and Louis—posed for a photograph in their gazebo on the ranch, with another photographer in the background. *Courtesy of the Elena Frackelton Murdock family.*

Symphony Hall was a center of Eagle Rock life. It housed Swan's Dry Goods and an early post office; upstairs was a community meeting hall. This later photo shows part of the remodeled Methodist church to the right. The Gateses lived in the house behind after their return until they departed for Florida. The building was later purchased by the Methodists for a parsonage and Sunday school.

then pursued grander plans. On the strawberry land, he laid out the Gates Tract in 1904 and the Glen Eyrie Tract in 1905, Eagle Rock's first and second subdivisions.

Gates left Eagle Rock in March 1910 to pursue real estate interests in Mexico and Florida. The family returned to their home on Caspar Avenue, behind Symphony Hall, in December and then left to make their permanent home in Miami. Gates touted his new land in Florida:

> *There are no mosquitos in the Everglades, a vast prairie of level, black muck soil approximately eighty by one hundred and twenty miles in extent, and there is no malaria there, no frost. There are few flies and very few insect pests, and probably as small a percentage of undesirable citizens or poisonous reptiles as you'll find anywhere in the United States.*

THE TROLLEY TO "SWITZERLAND"

In June 1904, Godfrey Edwards married Olive Rotha Hickson, the daughter of Mary Orchard Hickson. Mary Hickson's sisters were Ruth Parker, wife of Philip Parker, and Francis Jane Brierley, wife of James Alfred Brierley—all were early settlers with large landholdings. Edwards, along with Harry L. Winters, founded the Edwards and Winters Company in 1906, specializing in residential and commercial real estate. It operated out of a one-room office in the Laughlin Building in downtown Los Angeles, with a field office in Eagle Rock headed by A.S. Bourne.

In March 1906, with more than $125,000 in property transactions, it employed three people with six associated brokers, and the offices moved to a larger location. Otto G. Wildey was identified as the firm's secretary/treasurer. By the following year, the firm's ads proclaimed sales of $500,000 since the previous February and boosted Eagle Rock as the "Switzerland of Los Angeles."

Extension of the Los Angeles Railway to Eagle Rock in September 1906 facilitated rapid growth. A consortium including Gates, Parker and Edwards may have paid Henry Huntington $40,000 for construction. At the terminus, Townsend Avenue and Colorado Boulevard, Edwards and Winters built the first brick commercial block in 1907. The building was to house the Eagle Rock Bank, Water Company and Land Company.

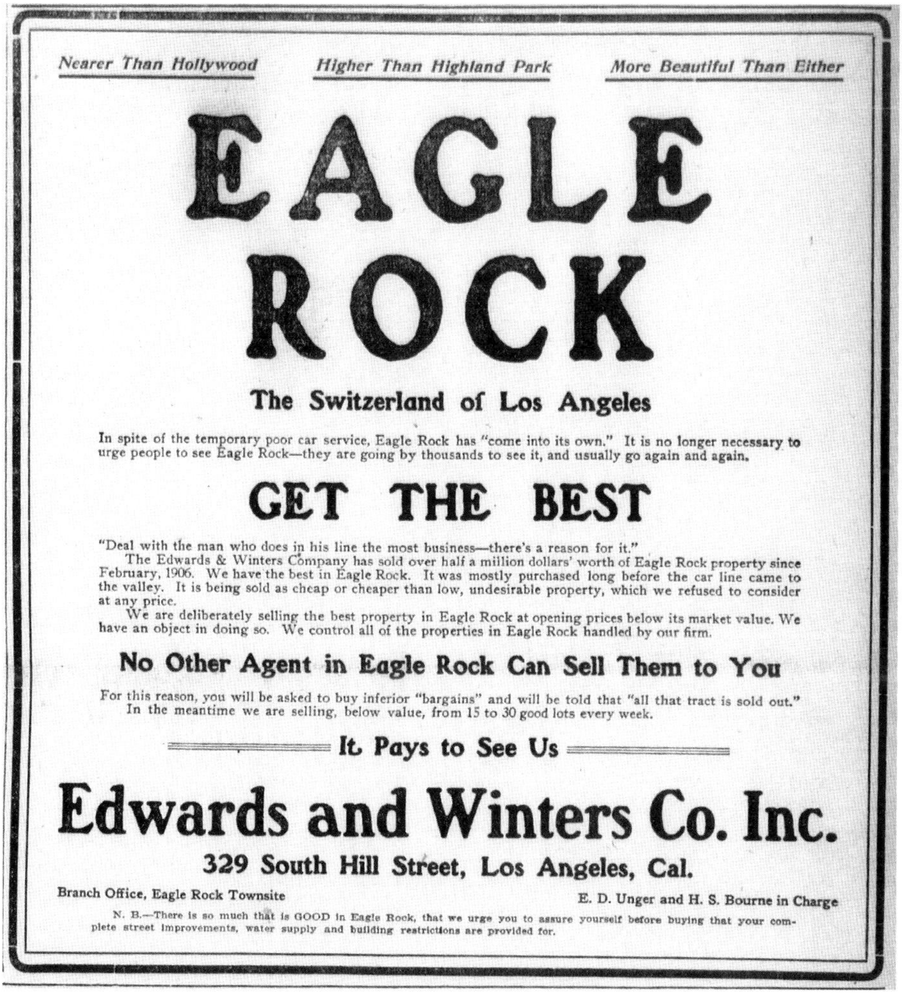

This real estate ad by the Edwards and Wildey Company heralds the wonders of the Eagle Rock Valley. *Published in the* Los Angeles Herald, *March 3, 1907.*

By January 1909, Winters was no longer affiliated with the firm, and it became Edwards and Wildey. From 1904 to 1910, land interests, lead by Godfrey Edwards, would record more than seventy-five new subdivisions, mostly consisting of five-thousand-square-foot lots. Only the steeper hillsides were not subdivided. Land speculation continued, but building on the land was slow. Edwards and others boosted the benefits of living in the valley.

In 1909, May Blumer returned to stay:

The Edwards and Winters Building sits isolated at the end of a widened but still dirt street. Behind the photographer is the Eagle Rock Road to Garvanza and Pasadena, small and unimproved. Long known as the Murfield block, it now houses Tritch Hardware. *Courtesy of the Elena Frackelton Murdock family.*

After some years and a trip back to Iowa I was back, married to a California boy and we began looking for a home, and I remembered the Valley and the friendly ladies of that day. And by then, there were many finished streets with a streetcar from Los Angeles along Central Avenue [Eagle Rock Boulevard] *turning on Colorado Boulevard and running to Townsend Ave. then reversing the seats and the trolley and retracing the trip…*

Usually it proceeded at a reasonable rate of speed so that riders from the north slope, hearing it grind around the corner could finish the last bites of breakfast and walk leisurely down to board it on its return trip. But when it was making up time it came back down-grade at a fast clip. And once (at least), it rounded the corner too fast and went over and skidded along its side. Luckily it was not crowded that day but some passengers were severely injured, including Mrs. George Kingdon.

Mr. Bourne sold us a lot above Las Flores Drive in the middle of a plowed field, and we built the first house on the west side of Central Ave. in that block. The street was graded and sanded and curbs and sidewalks were in. We had a mailbox on a post in front with an RFD No. 1, Box 88B address.

We had to use kerosene for cooking and lighting, but very soon had gas, which was greatly appreciated. Electricity came later. We deposited $5 for a telephone, which was promised when "a new trunk line" was installed but it was many years later that we had our first phone.

Coyotes howled in the hills nearby, and at times raided the chicken yards. The flowers and songbirds also were plentiful, as our ancestors had found them.

MASONS' HALL, COLLEGE INN AND MIRACLE CURES

Perhaps the most eccentric of early developers was James Ferdon. He made a considerable fortune as a "Medicine Show" man. *The Medical Council: A Monthly Journal for the Physician and Surgeon* reported:

James M. Ferdon who has traveled about the country under the name of Brother Paul and The Great Paul selling his so called Quaker Remedies and incidentally practicing medicine, was arrested in Chicago on April 6th at the insistence of the State Board of Health and taken to Freeport Ill. where he was placed in jail. Ferdon was prosecuted in August 1905 and judgments amounting to $1700 were placed against him. When about to be taken, he left the State. Since that time he has followed his calling according to his own statements in Iowa, Washington and California.

In 1907, Ferdon purchased Gates Hall and another lot across Maywood Avenue in his father's name and settled into a sedate family life with his parents, his son, his wife and her daughter, while still pursuing his profession:

Pasadena city fathers request suggestions of the best method of ridding the community of the presence of a patent medicine vendor who advertises himself an "The Wonderful Fer Don"...the city attorney will endeavor to recommend some way to prohibit the brass band and free minstrel show

George Diddock's real estate office was on the southwest corner of Eagle Rock and Colorado in 1909. Both streets are still unpaved. The side of the College Inn building is visible on the right. In the center right, the newly built Eagle Rock School is visible in the distance. On the left is the Los Angeles Railways trolley from downtown, heading for the end of the line at Townsend Avenue. *Published in the* Los Angeles Herald Sunday Magazine.

James Ferdon (left) stands with George Diddock in front of Diddock's real estate office. *Courtesy of Ricki de Kramer.*

attachment, which are the means of drawing the crowds of "gullibles" who buy what is purported to be "cure-all" remedies.

Ferdon saw the potential of the intersection of Colorado and Eagle Rock Boulevards early. Probably in collaboration with George Diddock, he purchased several lots near the southeast corner of Colorado Boulevard and Eagle Rock Boulevards. He first built the College Inn, which later housed, among others, the Sun-Lan Bakery Lunch and today, after reconstruction, Dave's Chillin' and Grillin.'

In 1911, Ferdon offered to build a meeting hall for members of the Masonic Fraternity residing in Eagle Rock, who were considering the formation of a local lodge. When the petition for dispensation was submitted, it bore the names of nineteen Masons representing sixteen lodges from seven states. By August 3, the group was meeting in the newly erected building.

The charter officers of the Masons. *Front row, left to right*: Godfrey Edwards, Worshipful Master Henry Elmer McConnell and Fredrick William Schneider. The others' names are given, but as they are listed only by office, the order cannot be determined. This portrait of Godfrey Edwards is the only one known to date. It is unknown whether Ferdon was a member. *Courtesy of the Revert family.*

The old Masons' Hall still exists on Eagle Rock Boulevard, with the parapet decoration removed and windows replaced. The Masons moved into a larger hall on Caspar Avenue. They were later consolidated with the South Pasadena Lodge. Note the trolley wires and unpaved street. *Courtesy of the Louanna Clark, Emma Young Collection.*

By 1908, Ferdon had traded Gates Hall for the Ringemann home in the foothills south of Yosemite Drive. His wife was the first woman to drive to the top of Mount Wilson, and his daughter rode on the Eagle Rock Float in the 1914 Rose parade. The family moved to Hollywood in 1914. After Ferdon's death in 1920, his widow, Alpha Staley Ferdon, constructed the building at the corner of Eagle Rock Boulevard and Merton Avenue.

Civic Growth and Promotion

The Eagle Rock Water Company was formed in August 1906 to serve the growing population by P.F. Schumacher, A.C. Helbrig, Godfrey Edwards, William R. Meyers, W.B. Judson, G.F. Morcom, E.C. Kulli, E.P. Hilliker and J. Winans. Water mains were extended from the Annandale Reservoir, and a second reservoir was started near Yosemite Drive and Eagle Rock

The Eagle Rock Water Company drew its supplies from wells scattered over the floor of the valley and pumped by this plant, located on the northeast corner of Yosemite Drive and Maywood Avenue. *Published in the 1909* Los Angeles Herald Sunday Magazine.

Boulevard. In 1907, the Eagle Rock Bank was incorporated with directors J.W. Eddy, Robert Henry Brown, Percy F. Schumacher, E.L. Blanchard, John B. Merrill, Godfrey Edwards and C.H. Barker.

In 1906 and 1907, the *Los Angeles Herald* chronicled an attempt by Eagle Rock and several other unincorporated areas to join the city of Los Angeles. Allegedly, the catalyst for this effort was City Engineer William Mulholland's plan to build an aqueduct from Owens Valley to Los Angeles. An article claimed that this was not the case for Eagle Rock:

> *Although many different owners hold the property in that district, the Eagle Rock Improvement association has prevailed upon all to unite in a uniform plan of street improvement. The valley's main thoroughfares are Central Avenue* [Eagle Rock Boulevard] *and Colorado Street. Both of these are traversed by the Los Angeles Railway Company's lines and have been widened to 120 feet each. They are to be oiled and tamped under the new "petrolithic" system. Hill Avenue is the valley's mountain drive; it is graded out seventy feet wide and curves in and out along the foothills, affording a never-ceasing*

> *change of view. All of the foothill tracts of Eagle Rock are being improved with streets ranging from seventy to ninety feet wide and bounded by beautiful wide parkways, planted to live oaks, jacaranda, acacias, etc.*
>
> *In another six months it is doubtful whether any other district in the city will show the uniform high-class public improvements of Eagle Rock. If the approaching annexation movement carries, the city will have no complaint to make in gathering up the beautiful little Eagle Rock valley, which in addition to her fine street improvements possesses a complete and satisfactory water system.*

The Los Angeles City Council called for an election on the issue. Two days before, the council adopted a resolution that the annexation of such a large area with few inhabitants "would greatly increase the burden in certain departments of city government, particularly the water department, the police and fire departments and the board of public works, at a time when the city is not prepared to provide for the necessities of the people in the new territory." It was "the sense of the council that it is not advisable that said territory be annexed." On election day, despite a low voter turnout attributed to foul weather, the majority of Los Angeles's voters agreed.

Necessary civic improvements continued. In 1909, Eagle Rock School District dealt with the inadequacy of the relocated and expanded old schoolhouse by building a new, larger brick building in the Craftsman style. The Annandale School District built a similar building for the new Rockdale School.

In 1910, E.D. Goode built the Glendale and Eagle Rock Railway connecting the freight and passenger railways in downtown Glendale to the center of Eagle Rock via Broadway and Colorado Boulevards. The name was changed to the Glendale and Montrose when the line was later extended there.

Elena Frackelton recalled, "When the car line from Eagle Rock to Glendale was built, old settlers were invited to ride the first trip, but the road up the Bessolo hill was so narrow, laborers had to go along with the car and chop down the hillside so the car steps could get by."

May Blumer remembered the single-truck cars of later years. "There was another short streetcar line, from Brand Blvd. in Glendale to Central on Colorado Blvd., which we called the 'Dinky.' This created great sport for young folks who would gather at each end bounce it on the rough spots until the extra rocking caused some sensitive passengers to get seasick."

On the crest of the rise of Colorado Boulevard near College View Avenue, the Glendale and Montrose Railway cars provided service to Glendale. "Pop" Nagle was the motorman. Before Eagle Rock High School was built, students could ride to Union High School near Brand Boulevard. The Bessolo house, built in 1910, stands on the terraced rise.

A rail spur and terminal south of Colorado handled much of the material necessary to build the new suburb. (The new Eagle Rock School and the rail terminal can be seen in the panoramic photo on page 122.)

In October 1909, two Eagle Rockers contributed to a pictorial section of the *Los Angeles Herald* devoted to Eagle Rock. The first, with the title "Life in the Valley," was by Howard Clark Galloupe:

> *Take the street car passing north on Broadway, and in less than forty minutes you will be ushered through the prettiest valley in all of California. Nestling here among the foothills—commanding an unobstructed view of the lofty peaks of Mt. Lowe, Mt. Wilson and Mt. Baldy—is the little valley of Eagle Rock just six miles from the business center of Los Angeles and forty minutes by street car…*

The Galloupe home was situated with a view of the Eagle Rock. The house was on what is now College View Avenue, then part of the southern extension of Hill Drive. *Published in the 1909* Los Angeles Herald Sunday Magazine.

In the fall of 1906 a few enterprising and far-seeing men of affairs, among whom we may mention J.A. Gates, Godfrey Edwards and others, began to realize that nature had made a setting here which could not be improved by the art of man. Acreage was purchased, streets were opened, the Los Angeles railway was induced to extend its line into the valley and then began the onward march of progress in the building of homes, which has transformed this semi-farming section into the most beautiful residence suburb of the city of Los Angeles.

The simple life of the country...is fully exemplified in all that has taken place in making Eagle Rock valley a center of beautiful homes. Men and women, true lovers of nature, many of them known as experts in the foreground of their various professions and callings...have brought forth other institutions that are a necessary part of a home community. A modern graded school has been established, and its educational facilities for the boys and girls are surpassed by few. The little wayside church, which for many years has been struggling for existence, has been strengthened, not only by those who are enrolled as its members, but by men and women of many religious faiths, who realize the necessity for and the influence of such an institution in a home center.

> *The women of the valley have organized a Woman's Twentieth Century club and are soon to erect one of the most artistic and complete bungalow club houses to be found in many a day's journey...*
>
> *Eagle Rock valley has a population of about 1000 people, two schools, a church, rural free delivery of mails every day, a commercial and savings bank, two stores where the necessaries of life may be purchased. While Eagle Rock valley is still in the country, and we wish to keep it so, yet it is not a country community. It is one of the choicest sections surrounding the great city of Los Angeles for the businessman's country home.*

Galloupe came to Eagle Rock Valley in 1906. In 1909, he would become the founding editor of "Touring Topics" for the Automobile Club of Southern California.

In 1911, after Eagle Rock had become a city, he was selected by the new trustees to fill a vacancy. As the chair of the Public Works Committee, his first action was to recommend changing the name of his street from Hill Avenue to Roca Vista. He also challenged the Eagle Rock Water Company's proposed rate and service price increases. The company was owned by some of Eagle Rock's prominent citizens, including his business partner Joy Winans. At that same meeting, the city attorney told the board that Galloupe's position was temporary. He ran to fill the vacancy but was defeated.

In 1914, while he was working as sales agent for Home Builders, the company was reorganized due to questionable management practices. Galloupe was discharged but ran for director and was reelected. Joy Winans was forced from the presidency, and Percy Schumacher was elected to succeed him. Galloupe was then appointed second vice-president. He chose Miss Jeanette Stortz as his private secretary and placed her in charge of the secretarial staff. According to the *Los Angeles Times*, agents of Home Builders alerted the city prosecutor. After a three-week investigation, Galloupe and Stortz were arrested in a downtown hotel room. Still married and living in Eagle Rock at the time, Galloupe disappeared from public life, and his name did not appear in print again until 1921.

CHAMPIONS OF CULTURE

Anne Hare Harrison was born in New York in 1879, the daughter of George Hare and Sarah (Hewitt) Hare. She came to California with her family at the turn of the twentieth century, settling on West Twentieth Street before coming to Eagle Rock in the mid-1900s. She married Arthur Waugh Harrison, a mechanical and electrical engineer, and in 1910, they had a daughter, Gloria. She wrote a series of children's books about a family of chipmunks called the "Wollopors," as well as a science fiction tale of a city built on the planet Mars. She was nominated by her fellow Women's Club members as a school board trustee. She introduced the Thanksgiving "Harvest Home Festival" to Eagle Rock School.

The Hare sisters—Martha, Sarah and Elizabeth—were active members of the Women's Twentieth Century Club and were deeply involved in the California suffrage movement. Ann's brother Alfred was pastor of the Eagle Rock Congregational Church, and her brother George Jr. was Eagle Rock City's first marshal.

By 1910, the Union Church congregation had outgrown the "Little Brown Church." Reverend Alfred Hare and other members of the community, including Galloupe and his wife, Mary, raised funds to build the Church of the Good Shepherd, known to many as the "Bungalow Church." The Methodists then left the Union and purchased the old church. Not to be behind the times, they remodeled it in the Craftsman style. Harrison wrote:

> [W]*e believe that no other place in Southern California can present to the artistic or cultured class of people the many advantages which Eagle Rock valley is offering every day.*
>
> *To the artistic it offers an endless panorama of magnificent views, of brilliant skies, majestic mountains, rolling meadows and wooded canyons. To the tired man of business it offers a quiet, peaceful home at night, where the few hours he spends away from his business may be spent in a pure atmosphere amid healthful surroundings. To the men and women who are raising families it presents the advantages of two splendid schools, thriving churches, a progressive Woman's club and a delightful social life…*
>
> *In a pretty little bungalow, at the top of a summer slope with her husband and a baby girl lives Mrs. Elsa Von Grofe Menasco, a famous violin-cellist. Possessed of a most charming personality Mme. Menasco had won her way into the hearts of the residents of Eagle Rock before it had ever become*

"Bungalow Church" is pictured at Maywood Avenue and Colorado Boulevard in 1909. It was known for its rose window.

The First ME Church stood on Colorado Boulevard, which has added streetlights and trees. The Methodists later purchased the two properties on Colorado Boulevard east of Hermosa Avenue for expansion. The Depression changed their plans, and in 1931, they rejoined the Congregationalists to form the United Church. The old church was torn down in 1949.

Madame Menasco was the first female (honorary) member of the Los Angeles Symphony. Her son was Ferde Grofe, arranger and composer of "Grand Canyon Suite." She returned to Eagle Rock to play a special concert for the opening of the Women's Clubhouse in 1915. She died two months later after giving birth to a daughter. *Published in the* Los Angeles Herald Sunday Magazine.

known that Mme. Menasco was an artist which the greatest American and European musical critics had delighted to honor. Mme. Menasco is a member of a family of fine musicians, her father, B. Bierlich, being first cellist of the Los Angeles Symphony Orchestra. As a pupil of Julius Klengel of the royal conservatory at Leipzig, Madame Menasco has gained for herself the plaudits of the musical world of Europe and America. And although the busiest of women, Mme. Menasco has yet a little time to spare for the Woman's Twentieth Century club of which she is a member and with her cello has generously contributed many times to the pleasure of the members and their friends…

Howard Arden Edwards, a young eastern artist, has spent the last two years sketching among the hills of Eagle Rock and has decided that no other charms can ever woo him away from the ever-changing beauties of our valley. Mr. Edwards' paintings have been on exhibition in the Blanchard art exhibit in Los Angeles recently. His tapestries are particularly beautiful, his latest one, "The spirit of Morning," attracting much admiration. His

> *little studio, which is built on a sightly point on the top of a hill, is open to the public every Sunday.*
>
> *Miss Floy Galpin, one of the best-known women educators of the country, has claimed Eagle Rock as her home for many years. Her picturesque home, which is situated on the western hillside, commands one of the most magnificent views to be had in the valley. Miss Galpin, who is one of the staff of the Los Angeles high school, is away on a year's leave of absence and is at present lecturing for the chamber of commerce.*
>
> *Mrs. Esther Zoline, a well-known miniature painter on ivory, has made Eagle Rock her home for a long time. Mrs. Zoline will leave for Europe in the spring to continue her work there, and on her return will again take up her residence in Eagle Rock.*

Harrison also described the early years of the Women's Club. "Throughout the history of the Women's Twentieth Century Club of Eagle Rock, our members have shown their capacity for creativity, resilience, resourcefulness, dedication and compassion. From decade to decade, we have met the needs of our community, our country, and other women. This is a legacy and history of which we are immensely proud." The club's motto is "Knowledge is Power."

> *It was on February 25, 1903, that a little handful of women gathered together in the home of Mrs. P.W. Parker* [Matilda Duncan Parker, his second wife] *and decided to organize themselves into a woman's club for the betterment of the social life in the valley. Thirteen members signed the constitution of the club, and, although there are but four of these charter members still in the club today* [1909], *it has steadily progressed until at the present writing there are between forty-five and fifty enthusiastic members, and the Woman's Twentieth Century Club of Eagle Rock valley has become well known as one of the most progressive woman's clubs in the state of California. Although organized at first chiefly as a social organization, they have taken up an important line of work each year, which has added greatly to the interest of the club work…The theme of study for the ensuing year will be "Woman," and under this head many important topics will be discussed. The hostesses will be the different members of the club. Many prominent speakers from Los Angeles and surrounding towns will also give addresses on this popular and ever-interesting subject.*

PART VI
EAGLE ROCK CITY

CITYHOOD

The services of the County of Los Angeles to an unincorporated Eagle Rock were limited to the paving of roadways and the recording of land transactions. Not much in the way of police, fire or other community services. While many residents were not satisfied, there were differences about how to best provide civic services to the growing community. Two community organizations, the Eagle Rock Improvement Association and the Eagle Rock Improvement League, were organized. While the organizations shared some membership, the association was composed primarily of local business interests, while the league professed to be residents seeking a voice in community affairs.

H.C. Galloupe, in an editorial he wrote for the *Sentinel*, stated bluntly, "The matter of incorporating the City of Eagle Rock has settled down to a question of, 'Who shall rule?'—the real estate interests in the valley or the private home owner. I must say that I admire the frankness of some of my real estate friends in stating openly that their interest in opposing incorporation is purely a selfish one." He went on to state that as residents of an incorporated city, the people would have say over water and tax rates and how the money would be spent on school and public improvements.

In 1911, this notice appeared in the *Eagle Rock Sentinel*:

The friends and workers for incorporation have secured Symphony Hall for Friday evening, February 24. The meeting will be called to order at 8:15 sharp. It will be a program meeting consisting of short, plain home talks, made by home people who believe that it is time to place the control of the most beautiful home valley in the world in the hands of those who believe in using home money for home improvements...An invitation is extended to every resident of Eagle Rock, whether he be on the fence or the ground. If "on the fence," come and let us assist you to come down on the side of the homeowners and the people who want to make Eagle Rock a good place in which to live. W.J. Cook, Chairman [Cook was the Chairman of the Eagle Rock School board. He then lived in the Broxham Victorian at Hermosa Avenue and Hill Drive.]

The issue was debated on page 2:

"Honor to whom honor is due." Every appreciative resident of Eagle Rock points with pride to the beautiful foothill and valley drives; and the unusual good judgment used in laying out the hill properties of our hometown. For this all thanks to the real estate dealers who have had control of this work. To the...Edwards & Wildey Company, is due the magnificent foothill boulevard known as Hill Drive...Designers of less taste and civic pride might easily have made these roads in straight lines, neglecting the natural contour of the country and ruining what nature intended to be a thing of beauty. The real estate firms have done their duty well as artists. They have been paid magnificently for it by the 1200 residents in the Valley. They are not safe as rulers. It is the turn of the people now. The committee has done its work well. Let us discharge them with thanks. (Unsigned)

POINTS FOR THE TRUSTEES

1. *Cut out the 75 cent service rate of the Water Company and give us minimum rate per month with equivalent amount of water for it.*
2. *We want better telephone service—fewer parties on the line and lower rates.*
3. *Establish fire hydrants and organize a local department for home protection.*
4. *Don't you think there should be some sort of inspection for plumbing cesspools and electric wiring?*
5. *Make the non-resident owner keep the parkways clean in front of his property and there will be more incentive for the rest of us to do likewise.*

6. *Put a muzzle on the pumping plants so we can sleep at night.*
7. *Compel the water companies to clean out the reservoir as often as the public health demands.*
8. *Stop the outside hunter from coming into our back yards and shooting holes in our screen porches.*
9. *Compel every resident of the Valley to deposit his money in the Eagle Rock bank. If he hasn't any money compel the bank to furnish it. (Unsigned)*

On February 25, 1911, the people of Eagle Rock chose to incorporate. A board of trustees was elected. The mayor was then selected by the board. The population was about six hundred. The borders of the new city were set by Glendale to the west and the outlines of the Watts Subdivision, with the addition of Campbell-Johnston's San Rafael subdivisions.

The following Wednesday, the *Eagle Rock Sentinel*, which had begun publishing the previous March, displayed an editorial by eighteen-year-old Franklin Schroeder:

> *It was a grave moment last Saturday night when the result of voting on the question of incorporating Eagle Rock as a sixth class city was proclaimed by the election officers. Thirty minutes' work—but the minutes seemed to be hours—and the counting of the 129 ballots cast by the voters during the day, was performed by the faithful election board, grouped around a table in the FerDon store building on Colorado Street. But equally interested in the important totals, pro and contra, were the boosters for incorporation. With pricked ears and sharp pencils, they sat and did their own little adding and balancing and when the last slip was taken from the urn, H.C. Galloupe sprang up and exclaimed, "Incorporation Has Carried," and his joyful statement was officially substantiated by the judges whose figures showed that 72 votes were cast in favor of the project, 57 opposed with the remaining invalid. So there was a preponderance of the progressives to the amount of 15 votes, and that difference, notwithstanding the fact that it is a small one, determined the future of Eagle Rock.*
>
> *...The climax of sentimentality was reached when, through the stormy and cold night, rang the bell in the tower of the Congregational church. As the old Liberty Bell once proclaimed the birth of America's freedom from the statehouse in Philadelphia, so Doc. Hare's bell last Saturday night announced a new era in Eagle Rock's history...*

Left to right: Charles W. Young, Wallace E. Bruce, Mayor John T. Bailey, William Keen Cowan and James F. Kincheloe, Eagle Rock's new trustees. None had lived in the valley for more than six years. They were in business and real estate. Bruce was later disqualified. The owner of Eagle Rock Drug Company had not lived in Eagle Rock long enough. *Published in the* Eagle Rock Sentinel, *March 1911.*

> *Vivos Voco—Mortuos Plango. I congratulate the victors, I feel sorry for their victims. Hail to the progressives, alas to those who have been defeated. Victory for the live wires, the dead ones have been snowed under.*
>
> *But when the last note sounded it seemed that the character of the music had somewhat changed; that the antis had suddenly protested to their burial; that there had been a resurrection of the dead and that there was harmony in the new born city and if another election were to be held the vote would be unanimous for progress and prosperity. The very men who fought incorporation will now be enthusiastic boosters for our city.*
>
> *The people are to be congratulated in their success of obtaining as managers of their municipal affairs such men as have been elected: John T. Bailey, W.K. Cowan, James E. Kincheloe and C.W. Young. As to the fifth place there was a tie between Messrs. Godfrey Edwards and W.J. Cook, each receiving 55 votes. An election will soon be held to fill this vacancy. There were further elected; City Clerk, J.S. Pitman; City Treasurer, Fred E. Biles; and City Marshal, George Hare.*

Outside the city limits, the citizens of Annandale and the trustees of Occidental College were leery of more local government.

OCCIDENTAL MOVES TO EAGLE ROCK

An issue in the incorporation election was the exclusion of Occidental College. When the county board of supervisors decided the boundaries of the area to be incorporated, Occidental was not included. The *Sentinel* reported in February 1911: "Protests against the incorporation as [originally] proposed came from Occidental College interests and others. A letter from President Baer…was presented backing up the protests (Unsigned)."

Letters were exchanged in the *Sentinel*:

> *In order that there be no uncertainty in the minds of anyone interested in knowing my position as regards to the incorporation of Eagle Rock. I wish to state that since the Board of Supervisors has modified our lines cutting off the Occidental College Campus and surrounding property; that I am very strongly opposed to incorporating what is left. What is the use of incorporating the rind—and leaving out the heart? (Godfrey Edwards)*

> *The locating of the new Occidental College so close to our borders is a matter of congratulation to the people of Eagle Rock. However we can not sympathize with the mawkism, fawning and obsequiousness shown by those who consider the college the "heart" and the five square miles of the beautiful valley to the north only the "rind." Possibly if we had been one of that select and appreciative company to whom was disclosed the "significant future etc." We too may have been willing to accept the rind theory. Notice we say "Possibly." It is never best to be too sure of oneself when confronted by great temptations. (Unsigned)*

Jean Paule, the college archivist, tells the story of the move in her biography of Occidental president John Willis Baer:

> *The community of Highland Park, where Occidental had secured land in 1898 and had begun to develop an attractive campus, was, by the end of the first decade of the twentieth century, evolving from a rural area into one of the city's highly desirable residential communities. Soon, however, it became apparent that the future of Occidental foretold a more spacious campus beyond the twenty-three acres in Highland Park…A major obstacle was the Santa Fe Railway that bisected the property adding insurmountable noise, and even a vibration factor, to what should be a peaceful setting for learning.*

Thus, the Board of Trustees in May 1909 unanimously adopted a motion to relocate…A committee of five trustees, with W.L. Green as chairman, was appointed. By September 1909 the site committee had a recommendation, namely seventy-five acres, located between Highland Park and the small community of Eagle Rock, in a beautiful pastoral valley. The land was offered as a gift from four local men—James G. Garth, W.A. Roberts, Ralph Rogers, and Samuel McCray. As terms were finally worked out in January 1910, the outright gift of the syndicate formed by two of the donors, Messrs. Garth and Roberts, was approximately sixty-five acres, and twenty-one additional acres were acquired by purchase for $13,500. In addition a gift of between two and three acres was made by the real estate firm of Edwards and Wildey, accounting for the approximate ninety acres commonly spoken of as the initial Eagle Rock campus acreage.

An ambitious "Occidental Park" tract had been laid out and was being promoted by W.A. Roberts Realty Company. Immediately across the road on the corner of what was later designated as Campus Road and Alumni Avenue Ralph Rogers, one of the four who offered the land for the campus, had his home. In 1913, as construction was being started on the three original buildings, he wrote a letter complaining about the herd of cattle on the campus grounds that crossed over onto his lawn. To Dr. Baer he wrote, "I do not think you want to allow a thing of the kind. If I recollect right, this ground was dedicated for the college and not for a cow pasture." He may have forgotten that two years earlier before any construction had begun on the new campus, Dr. Baer had to remind him that his chicken yard on the property adjoining the campus was in violation of covenant restrictions. In those days one never knew what problems could arise in moving a college to a new location.

Myron Hunt, one of the best known and most reputable architects of the area, by 1910 had designed a number of residences for prominent citizens, including the San Marino home of Henry E. Huntington, and was on his way to becoming the "signature architect of Southern California," as historian Kevin Starr has termed him. His "Mediterranean style" became his trademark and formed the theme for the Occidental buildings.

Dr. Baer made the announcement…to the student body assembled in the regular morning Chapel. Shortly thereafter the entire student body walked from their Highland Park campus to inspect the new site. As Professor William D. Ward, in his well-known poetic style said, "Spread out among the hills, with the mountains in the background and from the highest eminence catching an occasional glimpse of the sea, the situation is one of unsurpassed beauty."

The new Occidental College is shown in 1916. Fowler Hall is in the foreground, with Swan Hall and the beginnings of the athletic field behind. To the right of Fowler is Johnson Hall. In the middle distance are the trolley poles of Eagle Rock Boulevard. Eagle Rock City extends from the center to the right, where Colorado Boulevard can be seen through the trees. *Courtesy of Frances Moffitt.*

Reverend B.B. Wetherall, who was called in 1918, carried out the plan to erect this sanctuary and west wing. The Eagle Rock Presbyterian Church is shown here in an early rendering by architect H.M. Patterson. By the time of its dedication, Easter Sunday, April 18, 1920, it was more in the English Romanesque style. *Published by Eagle Rock Christian Endeavor Society, Occidental College, courtesy of the Stargel Collection.*

Back to reality, the requirement of the land donors that construction begin within two years caused considerable anguish as the trustees searched for funding. However, by the close of 1911, funds totaling $300,000 for the three essential buildings were assured, that is, for Johnson Hall of Letters, Fowler Hall of Science, and Swan Hall, a men's dormitory...

The projected occupation date of September 1913 did not materialize due to various delays. One problem encountered was discovery of an underground spring next to the Johnson Hall location, a matter so serious that it threatened abandonment of the campus. The problem was solved (although it had to be met again many years later when Norris Hall of Science was being built). Construction was far enough along, however, for the three buildings to be dedicated in March 1914 as part of the Quarter Centennial Celebration, postponed from 1912, and for Commencement exercises of the class of 1914 to be held in June. Finally classes began in Eagle Rock in the fall of 1914.

In the years between the decision to move and the dedication of the new campus, several important decisions shaping the future of the college were undertaken. An offer to join with Pomona College was turned down, a decision was made to make the management of the college nonsectarian while retaining the adherence to the tenets of the Christian Church and, most controversial, a vote by the trustees, in response to a request by President Baer, was taken to make the college a male-only institution. Female students, local and regional Women's Clubs and the public protested. The Presbytery of Los Angeles pointed out that coeducation was among the founding principals of the college and that considerable funding had been raised in accordance. After three weeks in April 1912, the decision was rescinded. Said Dr. Baer, "[I]t seems to me it may be possibly ethically wrong, even though legally right to adhere to our former decision, and I prefer to make a mistake, if one is to be made, on the safe side."

Inspired by the move, the eighty-eight-member congregation of the Bungalow Church decided unanimously to become Presbyterians, led by their pastor, Reverend Hiram L. Hoyt. Soon the pastor and fifty-five of the congregation rescinded the change. The remainder formed the Eagle Rock Presbyterian Church. Led by Dr. L.C. Kirkes, a strong pastor furnished by the Los Angeles presbytery and a professor at Occidental, the congregation met at Symphony Hall, purchased land and eventually built the English Romanesque Church that stood at the corner of Addison Way and Eagle Rock Boulevard until it was demolished after the 1972 earthquake.

St. Barnabas Episcopal congregation had incorporated in 1903. In 1913, it began to build its beautiful little church on Chickasaw Avenue, noted for its windows by Judson Studios. It is the earliest Eagle Rock church that stands today.

THE STATE HIGHWAY, HUNTINGTON'S SUBSTATION AND "EAGLE ROCK PARK"

Significant development in the canyon of the Eagle Rock began with the construction of parts of the state highway, which would connect the cities of the San Gabriel Valley with Eagle Rock and Glendale. Using some of the right-of-way granted by the Campbell-Johnstons in the 1880s, the road bridged the Rock stream on the high ground where the 134 Freeway bridge is today. The route came down Eagle Vista Drive and connected with Colorado Boulevard. The completion of the Colorado Street Bridge over the Arroyo Seco to Pasadena in 1913 reduced travel time from a full day to minutes. The rerouted and renamed Figueroa Street and Colorado Boulevard became major highways. The intersection of Colorado and Eagle Rock Boulevards became the center of commerce in Eagle Rock. The dual nature of the boulevards as main street and highway was born. This has been a source of prosperity and conflict until the present day.

Almost simultaneously, Henry Huntington built the "W" trolley line from downtown Los Angeles via Pasadena Avenue and Figueroa Street to Eagle Rock Park in 1911. He had purchased the land south of the rock ostensibly to provide a recreational destination for his line. Undoubtedly, he had in mind the development of the large substation located north of the Eagle Rock. Completed in 1913, it was the southern terminus of the Big Creek project, then the largest privately owned hydroelectric project west of the Mississippi. Power from the dam, one hundred miles north, would supply his trolley lines.

Helen Pratt wrote of her birding in the park:

> *Except for the stray cats, Eagle Rock Park used to be a fine place to see birds. There were good nesting sites in the old trees and in the native shrubs. There were trickles of water and small pools and seats at convenient locations of observation. We believe that the picnicking as it occurred was not a menace to the bird life. In fact many birds became tame and came for crumbs from the tables.*

The new bridge was hailed as both an engineering triumph and an artistic addition to the beautiful Arroyo Seco. *Photograph by E.L. Lewis. This item is reproduced by the permission of the Huntington Library, San Marino, California.*

The "W" line curves around the bluff on the south end of the valley of the Rock. Figueroa Street is on the left. It ran to the company-owned park, on Sundays only, until 1937. Figueroa and Buena Vista Terrace was the terminus on weekdays until the line was converted to buses in 1948.

Henry Huntington's Pacific Power and Light Company substation still stands behind the Rock. It is now part of the Edison distribution network, supplying power to the San Rafael area of Pasadena.

In this canyon the natural inducements to birds are many. In winter there are sunny slopes and also deep shade so that Thrushes who love the shade, rare winter visitors, are found here, and the sun-loving Golden—crowed Sparrows too, winter here.

Nelda Thompson wrote this profile for the *Eagle Rock Sentinel* on the occasion of the dedication of the aviary at Descanso Gardens to Miss Pratt:

Almost any kid who ever grew up in Eagle Rock remembers Miss Pratt. She taught nature classes at Eagle Rock Elementary; took them on "nature walks" at Camp Radford and Seeley. Hardly a youth group in the area didn't invite Miss Pratt to tell them about birds…and helped them win their "badges" and arm patches on the subject.

At a grown-up level she worked with the California Federation of Women's Clubs, teaching women the gratifying hobby of bird watching, and was always a popular speaker at her "home club," Eagle Rock Twentieth Century Club.

This postcard depicts the rustic bridge in the park about where the 134 offramp is now. Visible on the left above center is the highway bridge at the easiest crossing of the highly variable stream seen in the foreground. The stream still flows in the open through the Metropolitan Water District land, under the dump road and behind the commercial buildings on the east side of Figueroa Street, just below the 134 Freeway exit bridge.

Miss Helen Pratt's house is shown here, when new, with her sitting on the lawn.

Among her peers, the bird fanciers and ornithologists, she first served as secretary for seven years (beginning in 1921) with the California Audubon Society. She was named president in 1953. Her Junior Audubon clubs were sprinkled all over California, and Miss Pratt visited them often, keeping them up to date with the latest in birddom.

Miss Pratt's favorite sanctuary was in her own garden, one that she carefully laid out with an eye toward making the birds happy. That was back in the winter of 1913 when she decided upon Eagle Rock as the ideal home site for her semi invalid mother and herself. It was rural country then, blazing with poppies and lupine and birds.

Once settled in her new home in Eagle Rock, her days were filled with activity all geared to the outdoors. Those who remember her well, often comment about her boundless energy. She could crowd lectures, demonstrations, a study course and still have time to "bird watch" and write about her experiences far into the night; then up at sunrise, watching the birds have their early breakfast.

THE "BIG THREE" CIVIC IMPROVEMENTS

Francis J. Johnston wrote:

It was in the Spring of 1914 that the need for a library in the young municipality of Eagle Rock became so paramount that a meeting of those residents most deeply interested in the problem was called in the Hickson home on Hill Drive to discuss the matter. This group, the first library board, did more than discuss that first day, they actually composed and sent a letter to the Carnegie Corporation explaining the need and asking if any help could be given. After proper inquiry and consideration the Corporation granted $7,500 for the construction of a building capable of accommodating 8,000 books and for the purchase of a number of these books. During the period of correspondence and while construction of the building was in progress the Board made arrangements with Los Angeles County Library to maintain a few books for circulation in the dry goods store then in the Murfield Block.

By March of 1915 the original building was completed on a site which had been chosen by public vote only after a hard fought battle between east and

The Old Carnegie Library was constructed in 1914 after a spirited debate over its location. The books were initially from the County of Los Angeles. A controversy developed, and the county books were withdrawn. The library closed for a short time and then reopened with books collected from Eagle Rock's citizenry. Charles Lummis, Los Angeles's first librarian and Southwest Museum founder, spoke at the reopening. *Courtesy of the Security Pacific Collection/Los Angeles Public Library.*

> *west end factions each of which thought their end of town should have the new institution. W.E. Kleinpell was the architect; T.H. Addison was the contractor. On the night of April 1, 1915 the library formally opened; all the people attending the ceremony had to bring, as price of admission, at least one book. This resulted in a circulation of 1600 at the end of the first month.*
>
> *After the formal opening Mrs. Blanche Gardiner resigned from the recently formed board and took over the job of librarian, which she held for twenty-six years until her retirement in 1941.*

The second of the "Big Three" was the installation by the city of "42 beautiful three light ornamental street posts in the business center." The third had been in process since 1903. Anne Hare Harrison remembered it creatively:

Mr. and Mrs. A.S. Bourne are seen here heading west on Colorado Boulevard near the clubhouse. Bourne was the local agent for the Edwards and Wildey Company. Its sign can be seen behind the car on the land between Mount Royal Drive and La Roda Avenue. The arroyo stone gateway to Mount Royal Drive is at the right. *Courtesy of the Elena Frackelton Murdock family.*

The new clubhouse at Hermosa Avenue and Colorado Boulevard is depicted soon after its completion. Note the Edwards and Wildey sign on the left. *This item is reproduced by the permission of the Huntington Library, San Marino, California.*

The Women's Club meetings were cheerful affairs held mostly in the private homes, the church and the only empty store room (that one in the old bank building at the Townsend and Colorado Blvd.). A piano, chairs and dishes were purchased with funds derived from amateur shows given by the club members. Plans for a new club-house were discussed by the members on all occasions and finally the present site was decided upon and the Edwards & Wildey Co. and Mr. Edwards and Mr. Bourne were in charge of the building plans. Mr. Edwards went to England (in 1913) and Mr. Bourne was left to complete the building. [Actually, Edwards was in town for the completion of the building.]

One day he appeared before a small group of women with the words, "Girls, We'll have to do some tricks, to pay for the bricks." It seems that the building was complete except for the side entrance and $175 was needed to buy the bricks for the porch and the entrance that now opens into the dining-room from Colorado Blvd. No sooner said than done, and we did a "show."

It was a good show and it more than paid for the bricks. A crowded audience gave hilarious applause to the song hits, monologues and female quartette that sang feelingly "The Bird on Nellie's hat," and what was lacking in harmony was more than made up in "gestures."

The hit of the evening was a burlesque on a popular song of the time, which Mr. Bourne sang in a gusty baritone. It was a topical rendition of "That's Gratitude." Some of the verses ran like this:

When Edwards went to England, sure the folks got quite a shock—
They said, "That's Godfrey Edwards who sells lots in Eagle Rock."
...They took him out to Oxford
Their college site to see—
But he said, "Occidental,
Is good enough for me."

The club hired Frank M. Tyler, a prominent Los Angeles architect. The husbands of the members, all major contractors in the building of Eagle Rock, finished the building in six months on a very tight budget.

A celebration was held in December 1914, but the clubhouse and the library were still incomplete. The *Sentinel* narrated:

It was a success. That is the universal verdict of everybody who attended Eagle Rock City's first public celebration, on last Saturday evening. True, the weather-man tried somewhat to mar the evening's fun, and did keep some away, and cut short some of the social features at the end of the program...

The first on the program was the auto parade. This was in charge of [automobile dealer] *O.J. Root who was ably assisted by Messrs. Edwards, Young and Bourne. The cars began to reach the city hall at 2 p.m. and each was decorated with an Eagle Rock pennant, two large flags, and every third car with banners…"Eagle Rock Booster Night, Dec. 5th"; "Jubilee Singers at Eagle Rock's Celebration Tonight"; "Free Eats; Come," and other catchy words.*

The thirty-one decorated autos went to Pasadena via the new bridge, south to San Fernando Road, west to Glendale and then returned via Colorado Boulevard in an hour and a half.

Harry S. Bourne had charge of the speakers' stand, and no better stand and no better location could have been desired. It was facing south at the intersection of Central with Colorado, where the people assembled in the large open space. At 7:30 the Glendale concert band with twenty players started the program with a lively selection…

Mayor Galpin spoke on behalf the city, which has just installed 42 beautiful three light ornamental street posts in the business center. He briefly reviewed the growth and improvements in lighting and then spoke of the installation of the new lights here and what they mean in Eagle Rock.

The next thing on the program was a selection by the Los Angeles Jubilee Singers, a quintet of colored men who rendered several old-time Southern melodies, and the man with the prodigious facial cavern made much merriment for the crowd.

Mrs. C.W. Young…spoke of the "New Club House." She gave her version of what the letters in "W.T.C.C." mean, and closed with an appeal for continued cooperation and help to make the club and the new building of the highest good to all.

Another selection by the band and more music and fun by the jubilees followed, and then came the address of Godfrey Edwards on the "Eagle Rock Public Library," the third public improvement just now being completed.

The clang of the cowbell brought the crowd to the realization that the scene of activities must change from the platform to the lunch stand under the wooden canopy of the real estate office. There, Chas. A. Nash had arranged long tables, decorated overhead with evergreens and Japanese lanterns, and hundreds of red hot wieners, rolls and coffee were served. Everybody was "filled" even if it took a full half dozen to satisfy some of the small boys.

The Eagle Rock Sanitary Dairy truck. *Courtesy of Marc Henzel.*

Several organizations were noted for thanks. Pacific Power and Light, whose workers and new substation were supplying the lighting and power, and the "Mac Mullin Sanitary Dairy has the thanks of the Chamber and all the coffee drinkers for the gift of a large can of rich cream. It helped wonderfully in the taste of the coffee."

As much a sign of urbanization as electrification, the relationship of dairies with the city was complicated. Concentrations of cows lead to smell and flies. The dairy, owned by C.C. Miller, was first located on his partner C.W. Young's land in western Eagle Rock. The business moved east of Peyton Avenue (now Loleta) and then to the valley of the Rock, just outside the city. A 1917 advertisement reads, "Our equipment is new, sanitary and modern. We invite inspection. All milk is aerated and cooled before being bottled. All milk vessels steamed and sterilized before using."

SUBURBAN GROWTH

Construction in 1914–15 supplied many of the city's social needs. With World War I, the feverish pace of building slowed, but the population had tripled from 600 to 1,850 by 1916.

By the time Godfrey Edwards built the Women's Twentieth Century Clubhouse in 1914, his firm had expanded its real estate operation to properties in Glendale, Hollywood and Pasadena. In response to criticism of land sales without resulting development, the company subdivided the land, put in utilities, paved the streets and sidewalks and built homes ready for sale in Harvard Park (now Del Rosa Drive).

The company continued to prosper. In 1916, it built the Edwards and Wildey Building at the southeast corner of Colorado and Eagle Rock Boulevards at the heart of the Eagle Rock business district. In 1917, it built the new Eagle Rock School. At the height of a creative period in the 1920s, as Edwards, Wildey and Dixon Company, it built several buildings now

This panoramic photo shows the center of town in about 1915. Colorado Boulevard runs from the left center toward the valley of the Rock in the west. On the north side, we see (from left to right) the new library, the Eagle Rock Bank, Symphony Hall, the Methodist church and, several blocks away, the Women's Twentieth Century Clubhouse. On the south side, the trolley spur on the Glendale and Eagle Rock Railway leads to a freight yard. On the southwest corner is the clapboard office of Edwards and Wildey. Across Eagle Rock Boulevard is George Diddock's office, with Ferdon's College Inn behind. Just down the street is the Masons' Hall. On the far left is the 1909 Eagle Rock School. *This item is reproduced by the permission of the Huntington Library, San Marino, California.*

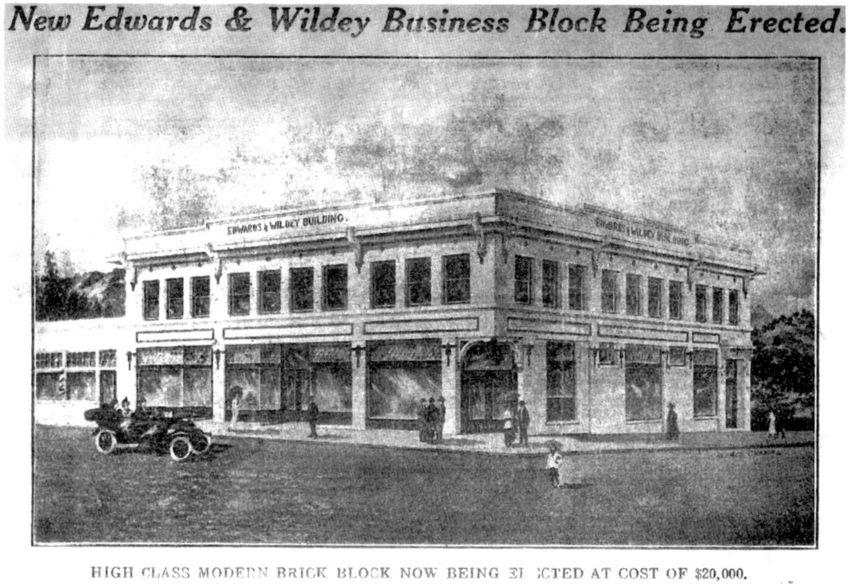

This 1915 architectural rendering shows the new, glazed-brick Edwards and Wildey Building. It was built across Eagle Rock Boulevard from its earlier, raffish real estate office. The building housed a drugstore on the corner until the 1990s; the soda fountain here was a hangout for young people between the wars. The building appears much like this, except for changes to the store façades on the left end in the 1930s. *Published in the* Eagle Rock Sentinel.

listed as historic: the Fine Arts Building, the Edwards and Wildey Building (downtown), Los Angeles Memorial Coliseum and the Shrine Auditorium.

In 1925, Suburban Estates Inc., a holding company organized by Edwards and Wildey, purchased Sunshine Ranch in the San Fernando Valley. They changed the name to Granada (later Granada Hills) and eventually marketed the area as particularly suited for raising rabbits. Edwards become ill and unexpectedly died in 1928. The company declared bankruptcy in 1931.

Another prominent Angelino moved to Eagle Rock and retired to his beautiful home on Colorado Boulevard. Colonel James W. Eddy, who earned his rank in the Civil War, constructed, owned and operated the Angels Fight Railway beginning in 1901. He retired in 1913 to be near his daughter, Carrie. He was a founder of the chamber of commerce and vice-president of the Eagle Rock Bank. His granddaughter, Purle Gillette, married Herman Hensel in the house, and they cared for him until he was "Called Suddenly Hence" in 1916. The house on the corner of Eddy Street (now El Rio) was replaced by the Model Market, which was, in turn, remodeled into today's Bank of America.

Colonel James W. Eddy's home was soon replaced, as well as the Craftsman farther along, by commercial development on Colorado Boulevard. *This item is reproduced by the permission of the Huntington Library, San Marino, California.*

Another new resident, Conrad Buff II, would raise his talented family in Eagle Rock. Buff painted the new library and won a contract to paint curb numbers for the city. Unfortunately, this displaced a more favored candidate, and Buff was maneuvered out. Eagle Rock historians interviewed Buff:

> [W]*hen he arrived here in 1908, "the valley floor was covered with apricot trees, many in a state of neglect as most of the small ranches had been sold to real estate developers." When the fruit was ripe in early summer anyone could pick it, as much went to waste.*
>
> *Buff was hanging some of his sketches for an exhibit at the Los Angeles County Museum in 1918 when he met Mary Marsh, a school teacher and a former art student from Ohio. In 1922 they were married. They built a house and studio on Linda Rosa Avenue, high on the hill. The studio was completed first and into this they moved on their wedding night, the house at that moment being roofless. Mr. Richard Neutra, the noted architect (the recreation building in Eagle Rock Park is a prize-winning product of Neutra), built the garage, retaining walls and the outside of the house. Buff designed the interior.*
>
> *Buff painted signs for Edwards and Wildey. The centers of these signs were red and had to be repainted quite often because the color did not weather well.*
>
> *In the early twenties his art work was becoming well enough known in the Southland that he was getting frequent commissions for murals in new buildings, both public and private.*
>
> *During the depression years the Buffs, Conrad illustrating and Mary writing, produced their first children's book, "Dancing Cloud." While*

> *staying with the missionary parents of Philip Johnston on the Navajo Reservation, the Buffs were caught up in the spirit of the area. Buff's inspiration to paint landscapes of the Southwest came when he and his wife made a trip to Zion National Park in 1925. He said it was the country itself that inspired his particular brush technique.*

Buff's son, Conrad III, would become one of the most prominent postwar Los Angeles architects. His grandson, Conrad IV, won an Oscar for editing *Titanic*.

May Blumer resumed her story:

> *We had one of Henry Ford's early "Model T's" in 1913, which had to be cranked by hand. My husband preferred the streetcar with the social visits with Eagle Rock men as well as to read his newspaper on his daily trips to L.A. This found me using the Ford to meet club and church speakers, gathering up flowers and greenery for decorations, running errands, so that I often missed out on the social visits with the ladies chatting together as they washed the dishes and tidied up the club. In those days while we were paying off the club mortgage we couldn't afford a janitor and caretaker.*
>
> *There were no movies, nor radios, nor television, or course, and only a few automobiles, but we did have phonographs with big horns. Besides birthday parties for children, whole families gathered on the lawns and porches for picnics together, with several blocks joining on the 4th of July and other festive days—and it was all very entertaining.*
>
> *Besides this, we had many plays and musicales, with sometimes talented artists joining. Ruth St. Denis and Ted Shawn had a home here and sometimes enlivened our efforts with their professional dancing and that of the pupils of their Deni-Shawn classes.*
>
> *About 1920 Mr. J.J. Broomall in his "Dahlia Guild" directed visitors to go two blocks north of the terminal of the streetcar on Rosemont Ave. to his Dahlia Farm. In 1924 the booklet stated: "The Dahlia Honored Again. The Los Angeles City Council acting upon the request of the Chamber of Commerce of Eagle Rock, has changed the name of our street to Dahlia Drive."*
>
> *Mr. Broomall was always generous with dahlia bulbs for prizes as well as giving his time and expert judgment when we had flower shows at the Club. He often named his new varieties for friends he wished to notice.*

Broomall would write extensively for the *Sentinel* and maintain his farming operation, the last in central Eagle Rock, until his death in 1937.

The "Dahlia King," Jesse James Broomall, was known nationally for his horticultural efforts. Dahlia Heights School and Dahlia Drive were renamed to commemorate this famous ranch.

While the community seemed to be well governed and prosperous under its own board of trustees, there was another attempt to annex the area to Los Angeles. In August 1915, the *Sentinel* reported:

> *About sixty citizens of the valley gathered Friday evening to discuss the question of annexation to the City of Los Angeles. It was sort of a private meeting held in a public place. A certain number who were supposed to favor annexation were invited. Other heard that there was some kind of meeting just "dropped in."*
>
> *John T. Bailey, the president of Eagle Rock Bank, chaired the meeting and started off by stating it, "was not a mass meeting but a number had been invited for the purpose of formulating...questions to be taken up at the next meeting of the City of Los Angeles Annexation Committee." The questions formulated were the usual on how being part of the larger would affect Eagle Rock's needs in terms of schools, water and sewer service.*

The "informal" meeting lead to a second meeting the following week that was attended by Los Angeles officials, including William Muholland, the head of that city's Water Department. Within the next three months, the issue of annexation was front and center in the community and would appear on the December election ballot, with the citizens of Eagle Rock opposing annexation by a vote of 298 for and 398 against.

May Blumer reported that the increasing population was straining the capacity of the relatively new school:

We had only a small elementary school in the present central location and failed several times trying to get school bonds voted (in 1915 and1916). Some of us were getting desperate and finally decided to poll the Valley voters and find out just why they voted against the needed schools. Day after day I drove to points on the outskirts with other young mothers, going from door to door. And sometimes the door was slammed in our faces when we mentioned school bonds. But we learned that a bond issue could only be passed if we had three schools to benefit east and west ends of the Valley as well as the more densely built-up central section. When the Chamber of Commerce acted on this information the bond issue was passed (in 1917).

Blumer recruited newcomer Alice Dirks Moore for the PTA:

I do not remember now who opened the meeting, but I remember well what happened. I sat there listening and soon Mrs. Hersom rose and nominated Mrs. Alice Dirks as President of the P.T.A. I was so stunned at first that I could not say a word but I finally managed to arise and ask "What was I president of and please explain, as I had never heard of the organization." I protested but the few women insisted upon my serving so I became the new president. I served from 1917–1918. We set about to get a kindergarten. I remember making many trips down to see Mr. Mark Keppel, our County Superintendent of Schools, and though he was one of the gruffest men I have ever met, he listened to me and he finally succeeded in getting our building on the grounds of the elementary school.

I think this was my first year on the [Eagle Rock] *School Board. At the first meeting each man had decided for himself that a woman would be handed the clerkship. This I refused since I was new on the Board...It was an embarrassing meeting with both men insisting, but finally it all ended with Walter Dorrance taking the job and Alice Dirks being made President. This staggered me but I made up my mind I could do it. I had the pleasure of presenting my son, Maitland, with his diploma when he graduated from grammar school. I remember giving my son his first gold wristwatch as a gift. During the summer he initiated it by going in swimming with it on. It was some time before he received another.*

Soon after taking office the teachers reported to me that we had many children coming to school without their lunches. They were hungry from the long walk to school, some even coming without their breakfast. Our P.T.A. set up a lunch program starting very simply—a mug of milk or chocolate or soup. This service proved a great success and later developed into the cafeteria.

Three new schools were built: East School, now Dahlia Heights; a new Central School (the building still stands); and West School, San Rafael.

Water continued to be a vital issue. Francis Johnston described the purchase of the company:

> *By 1916 Eagle Rock Water Company's equipment totaled four wells, two reservoirs, and several pumps. The most prominent mains formed a solid ring about the center of the town running along and joining at the junctions of Eagle Rock Boulevard, Yosemite Drive, Townsend Avenue and Colorado Boulevard. The wells of this system were about one hundred feet deep with an average water level of eighty feet. There were 25,000,000 cubic feet of water available to supply a consumer peak of 1,789 or an estimated average of 1,224.*
>
> *After incorporation as a separate city there was agitation among the populace for the town to take over the water system so in November of 1916 the Board of Trustees called for an election on the matter. $70,000 worth of bonds at five percent interest were to be issued if the election was favorable to municipal ownership. The Board also announced that should the company be taken over new rates would be established...The election was overwhelmingly for purchase with 569 votes for and 175 against.*

The growing population encouraged the development of more church denominations. St. Dominic Parish began with meetings in Angelo Bessolo's home. The first Catholic Mass was said in the home of A. Klein when a congregation of seventeen persons assembled. By 1920, the congregation had purchased land on Merton Avenue. Father Francis Driscoll offered Mass in a tent there on October 16, 1921. A few weeks later, De Porres Hall was under construction. The Seventh-Day Adventists began in a tent and had built a wooden church by 1922. That same year, the Church of Christ and the Church of Christ, Scientist, were founded.

The 1920 U.S. census count for Eagle Rock was 2,250. The *Sentinel* calculated using the number of households billed for water and then multiplied by average family size. It estimated that the population in 1922 was 4,500 people and that in 1923 it was 6,700.

The East School building stood on the corner of Colorado and Floristan. Classes were held in the Murfield block at Townsend and Colorado, as well as under a large tree behind it, while this building was built. It looks very similar to the West School and may have been built by the same hands. The building survived as a kindergarten until all the buildings were torn down in 1970. *Security Pacific Collection/Los Angeles Public Library.*

West School classes were held in rented rooms while this building was built. It was located near Broadway and El Verano Avenues, surrounded by open space. Elmer Lorenz is the third boy from the right in the second row in this 1920 class picture. A later building was demolished to allow construction of the 2 Freeway. *Courtesy of Elmer Lorenz.*

SYMBOL AND REALITY

Faced with the need to provide services to a rapidly growing city and the reoccurring question of disincorporation, the Eagle Rock Board of Trustees had led a peripatetic existence. The first meeting was held on March 6, 1911, at the real estate office of George Diddock, next in the back room of the Eagle Rock Bank and then in a storefront in the Welsh Building. In January 1912, the board accepted the offer of James Ferdon to locate in his recently completed Masons' Hall, where there would be adequate room for city offices and storage, as well as a place to hold meetings. In 1918, it moved across the street to the Ross Building.

Funding a city-owned building was put off until the early 1920s, when it was decided that it was time to build a proper city hall. The trustees selected architect William Lee Woollet, who presented an elegant Italian Renaissance Revival design that was a complement to its location, on a slightly raised site on the northeast corner of Colorado Boulevard and Maywood Avenue. Completed in 1922, just one year before Eagle Rock gave up its status as an independent city, the building would also house the city's fire engine. After consolidation with the city of Los Angeles, the building continued to be used for a variety of government offices and was also the home of the YMCA. Today, it houses the council district field office and remains a reminder of an independent Eagle Rock.

Consolidation with Los Angeles was soon again an issue. The dual crisis of water and sewage could no longer be ignored. In March 1923, under, "Private Citizens Give Their Views on Important Subject," the *Eagle Rock Sentinel* reported:

> *The campaign for annexing Eagle Rock by Los Angeles opened in real outburst last Thursday night, when the Central school auditorium was packed with citizens of all walks of life. The annexationists were in full charge of the meeting. No detailed program had been announced, and everyone who attended was uninformed as to just what would happen. We expected to get that side of it.*
>
> *John T. Bailey, always an ardent supporter of annexation presided…*
>
> *Mr. Bailey presented as the first speaker, Mr. Ralph Criswell, chairman of the Los Angeles City Council. He began by saying that he wanted it distinctly understood that he was not here to urge annexation or advise any attendees how to vote. He would only attempt to tell of how city business*

was conducted. He said, among other things, that they desired to effect a city-county government and when that was done it might be hard for outlying territory to annex. He spoke of how water and power had been developed for 2,500,000 people, and rates made lower than public utilities controlled by corporations. He stated the city officials would give Eagle Rock the same consideration as any other part of Los Angeles. He emphasized the fact that Sawtelle, having voted by a majority of two votes to become a part of Los Angeles; after four years was taken out by a court decision; then three months later voted by 6 to 1 in favor of again annexing, was good proof of what they thought of joining the big city.

Chief Engineer Knowlton was then introduced. He stated that the Los Angeles 18-inch sewer now at Glassell [Eagle Rock Boulevard] *and York Boulevard was large enough to accommodate Eagle Rock and this city could connect with it as soon as she put in her sewer mains at her own expense. He thought this could be done in about eighteen months.*

Mr. Moody of the Power Board, spoke briefly of light and power, of the low rates and also stated that Eagle Rock could have this service upon the establishment of a lighting system.

Mr. Bailey from the Los Angeles water department also spoke briefly on the water conditions in that city. He stated that a large supply of city water was furnished from the Los Angeles River, some Owens River water was also run into this. He said that the city was now laying a 24-inch water main south of York Boulevard, and no doubt Eagle Rock could be supplied from this source until the Tujunga high line was built, which would be about eighteen months.

Godfrey Edwards put some enthusiasm into the meeting by strongly insisting that there was now a shortage of water and it would be worse next summer; that the water was now contaminated. If we do not now annex, we will have to vote $150,000 in bonds to enlarge the water system.

A letter from Anne Hare Harrison was published in the same paper:

For the past eighteen years I have been a resident of Eagle Rock Valley. With the utmost love and affection, "we pioneers" have watched our city grow from a little country town of less than twenty homes, without gas, without electric light, without even a grocery store closer than Verdugo, to this busy little city of almost 7,000 inhabitants.

Our children were born here; our greatest happiness and deepest sorrows were experienced here. What wonder, then, if for sentimental reasons, we

In both panoramas, the intersection of Colorado and Eagle Rock Boulevards is at center left. Colorado Boulevard runs toward the Rock in the distance. Eagle Rock Boulevard, then Central Avenue, runs off to the left. In the upper view, in 1908, much remains farmland. Below, in 1923, Eagle Rock has become recognizable as the town of today. *Photographs by C.C. Pierce, 1908; graphics by Amy Inoye.*

1st Church Bldg.
Barber
Emmet Myers
Parker's Park
Palmer
The Eagle Rock
Gates Hall
1st Schoolhouse moved
EAGLE ROCK BLVD.
YOSEMITE DRIVE
Eckert
Dickinson
Capt. Lucas
Sherman
White
Stevens
New J. Q. Adams now child care
Galpin

Merry Go Round (waiting area)
Women's Club
Edwards & Wildey Building
Old Masons Hall
1917 School
EAGLE ROCK BLVD.
YOSEMITE DR.
Eagle Rock Lumber
Presbyterian Church

In 1923, the Eagle Rock Realty Board celebrated the "marriage" of Eagle Rock and Los Angeles in front of the Eagle Rock City Hall, which had been built only the year before.

> *should desire to keep our little town as a city by itself? But the time has come when sentiment and romance must give way to common sense and sound judgment.*
>
> *Eighteen years ago, there were less than twenty cesspools in Eagle Rock Valley. Today there are many more than 2,000. Our wells, which provide the drinking water for over 1,200 children, are in the floor of the valley where the seepage from these cesspools has already contaminated them…*
>
> *As mothers and fathers, it is our duty to set aside all sentimental or selfish feelings on the subject, and safeguard the health of the little children who are entrusted to our care, by voting for the only solution of proper sanitation—the annexation of Eagle Rock City to Los Angeles.*
>
> *Our students may attend many other high schools besides the one in Glendale, but there is positively no substitute for the Los Angeles sewer.*
>
> *This is a situation, which should be considered carefully, and a responsibility, which must be met fairly and honestly.*

On March 27, 1923, by a vote of 1,107 for and 810 against, the citizens of Eagle Rock voted to consolidate with the city of Los Angeles.

AFTERWORD

The concept and spirit of Eagle Rock would continue. The consolidation would put to rest some of the disagreements about regional development. Pasadena's annexations of land west of the Arroyo Seco in 1916 and 1923 would set the eastern border. Occidental would become annexed to Los Angeles in 1916 as part of the Occidental Addition but would continue to be identified as "in Eagle Rock." Citizens of Annandale in the valley of the Rock, with their Rockdale School, would increasingly identify as Eagle Rockers. The area would be annexed to Los Angeles in 1923. Parts of these areas would be included in Eagle Rock, as defined by the Neighborhood Council boundaries in 2002.

Eagle Rock High School was built in 1927 by the Los Angeles district as a neighborhood school, remaining a focus of pride to this day. Commercial and residential construction continued into the 1930s and picked up again after World War II. New people and institutions contributed to the community's vitality, but the "days of old Eagle Rock" were over.

SOURCES

Sources are listed in the order they appear throughout their respective sections.

Dedication

News from Native California 24, no. 4 (Summer 2011). Poem and biography originally printed in *El-Lay Riots: Memorias de Ya Town and Home Boy Poems.* Bandon, OR: Kahonkok Press.

Young, Mrs. C.W. "History of Eagle Rock Filled with Adventure, Romance and Politics." Article printed in a pamphlet by the Eagle Rock Chamber of Commerce, circa 1934. Biographical information by Donna R.M. Adams, Eagle Rock Valley Historical Society.

Part I

Cugno, Giuseppe. *The Geology of the Eagle Rock.* Eagle Rock, CA: Eagle Rock Valley Historical Society, n.d. Giuseppe Cugno lives in Eagle Rock and works as a geologist for the J. Byer Company in Glendale.

Johnston, Francis J. *From Piedra Gorda to Eagle Rock.* Los Angeles, CA: Westernlore Press, 1948–49. Francis J. Johnston wrote the first complete history of Eagle Rock while he was a student at Occidental College. It was finished and published in the *Eagle Rock Advertiser* after he had completed his wartime service. His research was aided by interviews with many local people. As far as is known, he was unrelated to Bernice Eastman Johnston.

Johnston, Bernice Eastman. *The First People of Eagle Rock.* Los Angeles, CA: Eagle Rock Valley Historical Society, n.d.

Salas, Andrew. Salas's views on the origin of the name Eagle Rock were transmitted to us via e-mail. His organization's views of the name for his people were aired in various leaflets distributed at historical gatherings in 2012 and 2013. The website for the Kizh/Gabrieleno Band of Mission Indians is gabrielenoindians.org.

Other organizations representing local native people include those of the Gabrielino-Tongva Tribe, a California Indian tribe historically known as San Gabriel Band of Mission Indians (gabrielinotribe.org) and Gabrielino Tongva of the Los Angeles Basin, Peo 'Tskome Tribal Council (tongvatribe.net).

Part II

Teutimes, Ernest P. Salas, Andrew Salas, Christina Swindall Martinez and Gary Stickel. *Toypurina: The Joan of Arc of California.* San Gabriel, CA: Kizh Tribal Press, 2013.

Kielbasa, John R. *Historic Adobes of Los Angeles County.* Pittsburgh, PA: Dorrance Publishing, 1997.

Perry, E. Caswell, and Carroll W. Parcher. *Glendale Area History.* Glendale, CA: James W. Anderson, 1974.

Cleland, Robert Glass. *The Cattle on a Thousand Hills: Southern California, 1850–1880.* San Marino, CA: Huntington Library, 1941. This history, by Occidental College professor Cleland, remains the definitive history of the era.

Welcome, Henry. "The Verdugos." *Eagle Rock Valley Historical Society Newsletter*, 1962–63.

Guinn, James Miller. "Alfred B. Chapman." *A History of California and an Extended History of Los Angeles and Environs.* Vol. 2. Los Angeles, CA: Illustrated Historic Record Company, 1915.

Part III

Guinn, James Miller. "Andrew Glassell." *A History of California and an Extended History of Los Angeles and Environs.* Vol. 2. Los Angeles, CA: Illustrated Historic Record Company, 1915.

Salvator, Ludwig Louis, translated by Marguerite Eyer Wilbur, with an introduction by Phil Townsend Hanna. *Los Angeles in the Sunny Seventies: A Flower from the Golden Land.* Los Angeles, CA: B. McCallister and J. Zeitlin, 1929. Available online at the Library of Congress–American Memory project.

Welcome, Henry. "Tiburcio Vasquez." *Eagle Rock Valley Historical Society Newsletter*, 1964.

Part IV

Los Angeles Herald. "Our Northern Suburbs." May 9, 1883.

Galpin, Cromwell. "Some Early Eagle Rock Reminiscences." *Eagle Rock Sentinel*, December 11, 1913.

Murdock, Elena Frackelton. "Family Album and Remembrances, 1886–1973." Unpublished scrapbook and memoir.

Murdock, Elena Frackelton. "Those Were the Days! Farm Life in Eagle Rock Told by Pioneer." *Eagle Rock Sentinel*, September 10, 1961. From a series of pioneers' memories compiled by Eleanor Zimmerman.

Swinnerton, Medora. *Eightieth Anniversary History of the United Church of Eagle Rock, Congregational and Methodist.* Los Angeles, CA: United Church of Eagle Rock, 1967.

Historical Narration, Seventy-Fifth Anniversary. Los Angeles, CA: Eagle Rock Presbyterian Church, 1989.

Los Angeles County, Department of Public Works. Online Land Records Information, October 2013.

Galpin, Cromwell. "Some Facts About Our Water Supply: Cromwell Galpin Gives Interesting Data on Eagle Rock's Water Source." *Eagle Rock Sentinel*, July 31, 1913.

Part V

Newhan, Beth Ellenwood. "Pioneers Found Refuge in Eagle Rock After Big Midwestern Cyclone." *Eagle Rock Sentinel*, October 5, 1961. From a series of pioneers' memories compiled by Eleanor Zimmerman.

Los Angeles Herald. "Organized for Protection: Berry Growers Prepare for Association." January 22, 1902.

Zimmerman, Mrs. J. B. "Remember When: Memories of Old Eagle Rock—Mrs. Edith Eckert." *Eagle Rock Sentinel*, August 6, 1961. From a series of pioneers' memories compiled by Eleanor Zimmerman.

Blumer, May M. "Honeymooners of '09 Chose Eagle Rock for a Homesite: Memories of Old Eagle Rock." *Eagle Rock Sentinel*, September 3, 1961. From a series of pioneers' memories compiled by Eleanor Zimmerman.

Los Angeles Herald. "Anxious for Annexation: Eagle Rock Suburb Residents Active in Development Work for Greater Los Angeles." December 16, 1906.

———. "'Cure-All' Vendor Troubles City Fathers." November17, 1907.

———. "Eagle Rock People Before County Board, Anxious to Incorporate—Population Exceeds 2000." December 11, 1910.

———. "The Board Was Petitioned by Ninety Residents of the Eagle Rock Valley for the Incorporation of About Five Square Miles of the Valley as the Town of Eagle Rock." December 20, 1910.

Galloupe, Howard C. "Life of the Valley." *Los Angeles Herald*, Sunday Herald Pictorial Section, October 24, 1909.

Harrison, Anne Hare. "Among the Hills" and "Women's Twentieth Century Club." *Los Angeles Herald*, Sunday Herald Pictorial Section, October 24, 1909.

Eagle Rock Sentinel. "Occidental Announces Building Plans, Architect Hunt and Gray." June 18, 1910.

Part VI

Schroeder, Franklin O. "Vivos Voco—Mortuos Plango: Schiller, 'Die Glocke.'" *Eagle Rock Sentinel*, March 1, 1911.

Swanson, Roger. "Chatsworth Man Published First Sentinel in 1910." *Eagle Rock Sentinel*, 50th Anniversary Edition, March 31, 1960.

Eagle Rock Sentinel. Series of articles and letters on incorporation, November 1910–March 1911.

———. "Supervisors Will Set Boundaries at Once: Occidental Is Not Included" and letters. February 8, 1910.

Cook, W.J. "Public Rostrum, Shall We Incorporate." *Eagle Rock Sentinel,* February 15, 1911.

Paule, Jean. *John Willis Baer, 1861–1931.* Los Angeles, CA: Navigator Press, 2000. Paule was secretary to the president of Occidental College from 1950 to 1965, secretary of the college until 1986 and volunteer college archivist from 1986 until 2011.

Thompson, Nelda. "'Bird Lady' Memory Lives On." *Eagle Rock Sentinel,* n.d.

Adams, Donna, Powell Greenland and Henry Welcome. Personal interviews with Conrad Buff II, *Eagle Rock Valley Historical Society Newsletter,* 1966–67.

Moore, Alice Dirks. "Pioneer Clubwoman, Alice Dirks Moore Tells Birth of PTA in Old Eagle Rock: Memories of Old Eagle Rock." *Eagle Rock Sentinel,* September 17, 1961. From a series of pioneers' memories compiled by Eleanor Zimmerman.

Eagle Rock Sentinel. Series of articles on annexation, August–October 1915.

———. "Annexation in Big Public Meeting." March 22,1923.

Harrison, Anne H. Letter to the editor. *Eagle Rock Sentinel,* March 22, 1923.

ABOUT THE EDITORS

FRANK F. PARRELLO has been an Eagle Rock resident since 1978. He and his wife, Heather, live in the Blackmer/Hull home, which according to a 1926 article in the *Eagle Rock Sentinel* was built as the model home for the Silverwood's Happyland subdivision. Frank has a Master of Architecture degree from the University of Michigan and was with the City of Los Angles Planning Department for twenty-five years before becoming the director of Planning at Historic Resources Group. Professionally, as a preservation and development consultant, he has worked on a number of preservation projects for the public and private sector, ranging from Historic Preservation Overlay Zones, Plans and Ordinances to the conversion of downtown's Subway Terminal Building to urban apartments, the rehabilitation of the historic buildings and the addition of new, affordable housing units at Christ Faith Mission in Highland Park.

Frank was a founding member of Highland Park Heritage Trust and has been on the board of The Eagle Rock Association (TERA), serving as chair of TERA's Preservation, Planning and Development Committee. In addition, Frank has served as treasurer of the California Preservation Foundation, is a member of the City of Los Angeles Colorado Boulevard Design Review Board and is on the board of the Eagle Rock Valley Historical Society.

ERIC H. WARREN is a native of Eagle Rock. His varied career came about through several experiences at Eagle Rock High School. He discovered through the theater that it is possible to be in many places at one time. In Mr. Born's photography class, he found that pictures are a window into the world for the photographer and his audience.

It became clear that graduating from Occidental College would be contingent on receiving credit for the time he was spending backstage in the drama department. He graduated with that major and went on to Stanford University, where he received his MFA in theater design.

His theatrical endeavors were crowned by thirty years of design for productions at Caltech. He designed many low-budget films and produced one for low-budget video. Union membership led to work as a set designer and art director in film, theme parks and television, most prominently an eleven-year gig on *ER* at Warner Brothers.

Discovery of the neglected archives of the Eagle Rock Valley Historical Society led to the restoration of the collection, presidency of the society and authorship of Arcadia Publishing's pictorial history *Eagle Rock* and its sequel, *Eagle Rock: 1911–2011*.

Last year, for Oxy's 125th anniversary, he designed *The Road to Eagle Rock*, a pictorial exhibit on the college's four locations in Los Angeles.

He is currently the president of the Kiwanis Club of Eagle Rock and a longtime board member of the Eagle Rock High School Alumni Association.